Praise for *Leading the Way*

MW01002378

"Are leadership books allowed
this is one of them. Compelli
learn on every page."

Mark Henderson, Chief Executive of Home Group

"Leigh and Maynard are leadership gurus. Combining a background in the performing arts, the experience of running a successful business for 25 years, and insights gleaned from working with some of the world's most experienced business leaders, helps them set out their thoughts on leadership today. They have big brains and bigger hearts. This is a great read."

Jason Gissing, Co-Founder Ocado

"Excellent leadership is critical in creating and sustaining successful organisations in all spheres of life. Anybody stepping into leadership in this day and age needs all the help they can get. This book is an invaluable support, full of practical ideas that are relevant to today's challenges."

Sonal Shenai, Executive Director The Funding Network

"I found this book insightful and immediately effective. Leigh and Maynard show how to draw on your personal strengths to develop the qualities of effective leadership."

Chief Executive, Trayport Limited

"The charitable sector needs strong quality leadership just as much as the corporate sector, but charities rarely have much of a budget to spend on training. Practical, discerning as well as intuitive, this book is inspiring as well as encouraging. Leigh and Maynard know what they're talking about and draw on many years of experience. This book should definitely be on the reading list of aspiring and established Chief Executives."

Francesca Roberts – Chief Executive at CRASH

Leading the Way

PEARSON

At Pearson, we believe in learning – all kinds of learning for all kinds of people. Whether it's at home, in the classroom or in the workplace, learning is the key to improving our life chances.

That's why we're working with leading authors to bring you the latest thinking and the best practices, so you can get better at the things that are important to you. You can learn on the page or on the move, and with content that's always crafted to help you understand quickly and apply what you've learned.

If you want to upgrade your personal skills or accelerate your career, become a more effective leader or more powerful communicator, discover new opportunities or simply find more inspiration, we can help you make progress in your work and life.

Pearson is the world's leading learning company. Our portfolio includes the Financial Times, Penguin, Dorling Kindersley, and our educational business, Pearson International.

Every day our work helps learning flourish, and wherever learning flourishes, so do people.

To learn more please visit us at: **www.pearson.com/uk**

Leading the Way

The Seven Skills to Engage, Inspire and Motivate

Andrew Leigh and Michael Maynard

PEARSON

Harlow, England • London • New York • Boston • San Francisco • Toronto • Sydney • Auckland • Singapore • Hong Kong
Tokyo • Seoul • Taipei • New Delhi • Cape Town • São Paulo • Mexico City • Madrid • Amsterdam • Munich • Paris • Milan

PEARSON EDUCATION LIMITED

Edinburgh Gate
Harlow CM20 2JE
Tel: +44 (0)1279 623623
Fax: +44 (0)1279 431059
Website: www.pearson.com/uk

First published in Great Britain in 2012

© Andrew Leigh and Michael Maynard 2012

The right of Andrew Leigh and Michael Maynard to be identified as authors of this work has been asserted by them in accordance with the Copyright, Designs and Patents Act 1988.

Pearson Education is not responsible for the content of third-party internet sites.

ISBN: 978-0-273-77680-2

British Library Cataloguing-in-Publication Data
A catalogue record for this book is available from the British Library

Library of Congress Cataloging-in-Publication Data
A catalog record for this book is available from the Library of Congress

All rights reserved. No part of this publication may be reproduced, stored in a retrieval system, or transmitted in any form or by any means, electronic, mechanical, photocopying, recording or otherwise, without either the prior written permission of the publisher or a licence permitting restricted copying in the United Kingdom issued by the Copyright Licensing Agency Ltd, Saffron House, 6–10 Kirby Street, London EC1N 8TS. This book may not be lent, resold, hired out or otherwise disposed of by way of trade in any form of binding or cover other than that in which it is published, without the prior consent of the Publishers.

***The Financial Times*. With a worldwide network of highly respected journalists, *The Financial Times* provides global business news, insightful opinion and expert analysis of business, finance and politics. With over 500 journalists reporting from 50 countries worldwide, our in-depth coverage of international news is objectively reported and analysed from an independent, global perspective. To find out more, visit www.ft.com/pearsonoffer**

10 9 8 7 6 5 4 3 2 1
16 15 14 13 12

Typeset in 10/15 ITC Giovanni Std by 3
Printed and bound in Great Britain by Ashford Colour Press, Gosport

Contents

About the authors xi

Acknowledgements xiii

Introduction xv

Leading in the twenty-first century 1
- Major trends 5
- Living with uncertainty 7
- Leadership is relational 8
- Leadership starts here! 12

01 Individuality 17
- The genius syndrome 20
- What price charisma? 22
- The source of individuality 23
  - Being yourself 24
  - Personal experience 26
  - Personal style 28
- Personal values 32
- Integrity 35
  - Integrity barometer 37
  - Taking a stand 38
- Networking 38
- Summary and ideas for action 40

02 Insight 43
- Self-awareness 46
  - Personal enquiry 50
  - Internal cast 51
- Understanding other people 52
- Seeing what's going on 56

- Fighting the filters 58
- Curiosity 59
- Foresight 61
- Insight is seeing, not magic 63

■ Summary and ideas for action 63

03 Initiate 67

■ Accept responsibility 72
- Volunteer 73
- Participate 73
- Be accountable 74
- Take centre stage 75

■ Research 75

■ Take risks 77
- Step out of your comfort zone 78
- Be assertive 81
- Handle reverses 81

■ Instigate direct action 82

■ Follow through 84

■ Summary and ideas for action 86

04 Involve 89

■ Participation and enrolment 94

■ Why engage? 97

■ How to engage people 98
- Being valued 98
- Being involved 100
- Being developed 101
- Being inspired 101

■ Meetings 101

■ Empowerment 104

■ Coaching 106

■ Giving people a voice 109

■ Summary and ideas for action 112

05 Inspire 115
- How to inspire 119
  - The why? 120
  - Sources of inspiration 120
  - Passion 122
- Vision 124
- Communication 128
  - Conversation 130
  - Story-telling 130
- Trust 131
- Challenging goals 132
- Summary and ideas for action 133

06 Improvise 135
- The drive for improvisation 138
- Principles of improvisation 142
- Creativity 145
  - Innovation 146
  - A 'try it' environment 148
  - Problem-solve 151
  - Value ideas 153
  - Encourage play 154
- Flexibility 156
- Presence 157
  - Physical presence 158
  - Psychological presence 160
- Summary and ideas for action 161

07 Implement 163
- Be action-minded 167
  - Paralysis of analysis 167
  - Setting goals 169
  - SMART goals 171
  - Monitoring progress 173
  - Ask for help 174

- Model behaviour 175
- Seek feedback 177
  - Personal feedback 178
  - Organisational feedback 179
- Persist 179
- Spot success 182
- Well-being 183
- Summary and ideas for action 184

Lead the way – *now!* 187

Overview 191

Are you leading the way? 193

Recommended reading 199

Index 201

About the authors

Andrew Leigh is author of over a dozen books on management, many translated around the world, as well as a regular contributor to the 'Straight Talking' blog on the HR Zone website. His publications deal with teams, leadership, presenting, change, communication, decision-making, and most recently charisma.

Andrew originally trained as an economist, he has an MA in the field of Human Resources, and is a Chartered Fellow of the Chartered Institute of Personnel and Development.

Andrew started his working career in marketing, later joining The Observer newspaper as a business feature writer. His regular newspaper column on Social Services led to a natural move into local government, where he established and managed a large research and development unit in a London local authority. On becoming Assistant Director of Social Work, he led a diverse range of teams, concluding his period in the public sector by setting up and managing a large Adult Service division with over 1000 staff and numerous residential homes and day centres.

With his fellow director Michael Maynard, Andrew founded Maynard Leigh Associates in 1989, now a leading UK development company specialising in helping clients achieve behavioural change, at the individual, team and corporate levels. As a consultant, Andrew advises companies on creating effective people development programmes, particularly ones dealing with cultural change.

Michael Maynard originally studied sociology before becoming a professional actor, scriptwriter and presenter for nearly 20 years, working in theatre, Radio and TV. He started Maynard Leigh Associates in 1989 with his fellow director Andrew Leigh and a team of talented consultants.

Michael has run business and management courses internationally, specialising in leadership and creativity, teams and communication skills. He has worked with thousands of people at all levels of management, to improve their personal effectiveness and communication skills, including senior executives from companies such as: Barclays, Cancer Research UK, Cisco, DHL, Hewlett Packard, Lloyds, London Stock Exchange, SES and T-Mobile.

Together with Andrew Leigh he has written several books: *Dramatic Success* and *Leading Your Team* (Nicholas Brealey Publications) *ACE Teams – Creating Star Performance In Business* (Butterworth Heinemann) and three in the Random House Perfect Management Series on Presentation, Communication and Leadership.

Michael regularly presents conferences all over the world on Teams, Leadership, Creativity and Innovation, Unlocking Potential, Communication and Sales Motivation. He is also the Chair of a charitable organisation that connects a network of philanthropists to progressive social change projects.

Authors' acknowledgements

This book strongly argues that leadership is about relationships. And relationships are also vital to us during the process of writing. We are deeply grateful to our wives, Gillian and Carol, for their encouragement and willingness to sustain our relationships, especially when we are pre-occupied by meeting deadlines.

We also owe a huge debt to all the people at Maynard Leigh Associates – they allow us to practise and develop our own leadership on a daily basis. The workshop leaders, coaches and consultants there have all helped us deepen our understanding of the seven leadership skills highlighted in this book, and illustrated their practical application in the workplace.

Getting anything done, without these relationships, would be impossible.

Publisher's acknowledgements

We are grateful to the following for permission to reproduce copyright material:

Page 4, Table 'The changing leadership landscape' expanded from R. Adler, *Leveraging the Talent-Driven Organization*, The Aspen Institute, 2010, reproduced with permission. Page 141, Table 'How improvising helps leadership performance', adapted from The Center for Creative Emergence, www.creativeemergence.com, reproduced with permission.

In some instances we have been unable to trace owners of copyright material, and would appreciate any information that would enable us to do so.

Introduction

The world is full of leaders. They are everywhere, yet we are manifestly short of leadership. In today's organisations it seems fair to talk of a crisis of leadership. There is mounting evidence of far too many people at work feeling alienated, disengaged and spiritually unrewarded by their work environment. Why?

Although the world is clearly changing, leadership is failing to keep up. While leaders regularly change their cars, computers or mobile phones, they are far less ready to adjust their leadership style. Some still cling to the notion of hierarchy and rely on command and control in a world that is loudly demanding agility, empowerment and speed of response.

While leadership matters more now than ever, and while more money is spent seeking the 'true' attributes of successful leaders, the quality of leadership continues to be a significant concern throughout the world. In numerous surveys when executives are asked what is required for firms to succeed in the future, leadership tops the list. Somehow the investment in developing better leaders seems to be missing the desired impact.[1]

This book describes the essential components of successful leadership in the twenty-first century. No one can know these for sure of course, until after the event. We claim no exceptional powers of prediction. However, working with leaders and focusing on their development as we have done over the years, it seems apparent that even the most successful organisations need a new approach and a revised skill set. We call two of these skills **foundations**,

[1] See, for example, Jim Intagliata, Dave Ulrich and Norm Smallwood, 'Leveraging leadership competencies to produce leadership brand: creating distinctiveness by focusing on strategy and results', *Human Resources Planning*, 23(4) 12–23.

specifically: **individuality** and **insight**. These, together with five other **capabilities**, are likely to be seen as essential in the coming years, regardless of industry, type of business or organisation.

We are attempting to change how people think and talk about leadership. Rather than basing future development on what may well be outdated and irrelevant assumptions, we aim here to reflect forces that are already shaping organisations. These and others we can barely glimpse over the horizon offer important clues as to what leading will mean in practice.

We cannot ignore the warning signs that leadership needs a fresh approach. There are many reports of low levels of staff engagement and trust, absenteeism and lack of diversity, leading to poor levels of innovation and creative thinking and weak performance management. The Chartered Institute of Personnel and Development (CIPD), for instance, found it necessary recently to produce a report solely devoted to the issue of trust, running to over 100 pages of detailed facts and arguments.[2]

A new approach is therefore essential because astute organisations are increasingly realising that if they do what they have always done in developing their leaders they are only likely to get more of the same. And yet more of the same is almost certainly not what most twenty-first-century organisations will need. They will require people who can make sense of the ever-increasing complexity of organisations, who can live comfortably with uncertainty and ambiguity, and manage risk with courage and confidence.

> "The tragedy of life is that we understand it backwards – but we have to live it forwards."
>
> **Søren Kierkegaard, philosopher**

[2] Chartered Institute of Personnel and Development, 'Where has all the trust gone?', 1 March 2012.

If you are already a leader, or are aspiring to be one, this book is aimed at you, not an academic audience. Here you will come face to face with the factors that will make a difference in shaping your leadership development, and advice on how to turn these into practical action. While you may not agree with everything we present here, at least it's a provocative starting point for deciding what you *do* need to do in this area.

After reading this book, you will have a clearer view on what it will take to be *leading the way* in the twenty-first century, or how to survive and sustain your effectiveness if you are already doing so. It is not a cookbook with a sure-fire recipe for how to lead. It is more of a route map for becoming a sustainable leader. Follow it and you are likely to be around longer than many unfortunate colleagues who remain stuck with increasingly outmoded leadership behaviours.

We offer you processes, stories and examples to help clarify what it means to *lead the way*. Even so, the rate of change and increasing uncertainty means it is impossible to lay down the law about the exact nature of the new style of leadership. It is constantly emerging. This is why this book is a route map and not a recipe.

Finally, what – if anything – makes us qualified to talk about what you need to do in order to lead effectively in the current climate and into the future?

First, for over two decades unlocking leadership potential has dominated our radar. For example, our company Maynard Leigh Associates has worked with a wide variety of national and global organisations to develop both their existing and future leaders. Along the way we have witnessed many other attempts to develop new leadership behaviour, many of which have failed or lacked sustainability. This book incorporates many of the lessons drawn from what we have seen, and from our practical experience of creating programmes that generate actual sustained behavioural change.

Second, our particular perspective on human and leadership behaviour reflects our pioneering use of theatre ideas in business. Once, these seemed fanciful. Yet as anyone who studies leaders soon realises, successful leaders rely heavily on techniques and methods that indeed make them 'performers' in every sense of the word. Whatever else changes about the leadership role in the coming years, we remain convinced that the successful leaders will continue to need this performance capability.

Finally, for nearly a quarter of a century we have led our own company, Maynard Leigh Associates, through some extremely tough commercial times. Like steel tempered in a furnace, this practical experience has tested us both individually and as an organisation. Our views and application of leadership therefore spring from a reality often lacking in books of this kind. Frankly, we know from personal experience just how tough it is to lead, and therefore continue to evolve our own view of what it will take to succeed as a twenty-first-century leader.

Leading in the twenty-first century

Leadership is about both the person and the context. Most of this book is about the first part of that statement – you and the capabilities you will need in order to be effective. Nevertheless, we need to take a little time exploring the other element that will affect you – the environment in which you are operating. So let us take a look at the context.

To make sense of how you will need to lead we must have some idea of what a successful twenty-first-century organisation might look like. Despite the mass of research and evidence, building this picture is no easy matter. Before our eyes, organisational capabilities and the context in which they operate keep changing and new notions about what a successful organisation might look like are constantly emerging. Wherever you are as a leader, you must respond to key trends, often mega ones. Any one of these could have major implications for your leadership.

For instance, you can expect the boundaries between work and personal activities to become increasingly blurred over the next decade. The assumed norm is to be 24/7 mobile and have high levels of connectivity. This has huge implications for your leadership if you are to draw the best from yourself and others. It will affect your daily leadership choices. For instance, you will probably need to adopt more flexible and agile working patterns, reduce hierarchies and move to more virtual work communities, perhaps even operating out of different countries.

These trends pose new conflicts and questions about where power lies within your organisation, such as how to harness technology to involve and engage people. Such issues were slowly surfacing towards the end of the twentieth century. They are now increasingly making themselves felt in many quarters and, as a leader, you need to actively address them. An intellectual response is not enough. Somehow awareness of all these factors must translate into the way you lead. The table compares the key characteristics of a typical twentieth-century organisation with those of a successful twenty-first-century organisation.

The changing leadership landscape

Twentieth-century organisation	Twenty-first-century organisation
Vertically integrated	Horizontally networked
Top-down leadership	Distributed responsibility
Build the ultimate product	Continuous improvement
Gain efficiency	Scale learning
Hoard information/build intellectual property	Share information
Experts	Learning new skills
Lone hero	High-performance teams
Security	Transparency
Push to change	Pull towards change
Goal-centric	Talent-centric
Risk-aversive	Risk-tolerant
Build systems	Build relationships
Get everything clear	Good-enough vision
Be sure	Paradox
Seek simplicity	Accept complexity
Ignore pessimists	Shadow side
Big-bang solutions	Link simple systems
Leveraging size	Leveraging learning
Technology-aware	Technology-pervasive
Demographically-aware	Diversity rules
Networking	Connected
Instructing	Collaborating

Source: Expanded from R. Adler, *Leveraging the Talent-Driven Organization*, The Aspen Institute, 2010, reproduced by permission.

No longer can you view organisations as machines. Instead they are living and breathing organisms – unpredictable and multifaceted. These twenty-first-century organisations have been given a suitably confusing title by organisational scientists: complex adaptive systems. That means they are systems that are extremely complex and subject to constant change and adaptation.

Despite their complexity, the broad outlines of such systems are clear. In them uncertainty rules and, where leadership exists, it is equally fluid, with authority and influence reliant on rather different forces than those faced by leaders in the past. For example, modern organisations are more easily compared to flocks of geese than machines, in which the lead bird constantly changes, to be replaced by another and another. In the future, a leader may be someone who comes from anywhere in the organisation, emerging, perhaps only temporarily, in response to the ever-altering landscape.

Major trends

To make sense of these complex adaptive systems you will need to recognise the five mega forces busily transforming what past leaders once took for granted about work:[1]

- accelerating globalisation
- technology
- demography
- societal changes
- climate change and a shift to a low-carbon economy.

Mega forces are long-term transformations on a worldwide scale that have a dramatic impact. They can be observed over decades

[1] See, for example, Jeffrey S. Nielsen, *The Myth of Leadership: Creating Leaderless Organizations*, Intercultural Press, 2004.

and projected with reasonable probability at least 15 years ahead. Successful organisations will be those able to ride the waves of these forces, turning them to their advantage and relying on a new type of leader. Many organisations will need to radically adapt their cultures, structures, systems and processes to survive the new work environment. Above all, they will need a new form of leadership.

For example, the once-dominant myth of the sole heroic leader continues to erode in the face of strong evidence that such leadership is hard to replicate, unrealistic, and not what is needed in the chaotic environment in which most organisations must now operate. As a post-heroic leader you will therefore be different from your earlier counterparts.

To survive as a leader in the twenty-first century, especially in a large organisation, you can no longer expect to command and give direction by relying on a highly centralised, hierarchical bureaucracy. Instead, success will depend on teams, ever-changing alliances, networking, and working through collaboration. Rather than relying on authority to get things done, you will depend on your ability to stay connected.

In twenty-first-century organisations that have a long-term future, leadership will increasingly appear from anywhere and profoundly affect what goes on and why. For example, you can expect to be part of a talent-driven organisation in which leaders emerge to assist with creativity, handle transitions, deal with turbulence, and respond to the need for both individuals and the enterprise to constantly adapt. Later these 'temporary' leaders may simply return to their previous non-leadership roles.

In such a personally challenging environment you will need to rely on two fundamental aspects of leadership: your **individuality** and your **insight**. Like a talented stage director, you will be conjuring up the equivalent of a three-act play, without a script and relying entirely on the abilities of an often sceptical and sometimes changing cast of actors. Still want to *lead the way*?

Living with uncertainty

The ability to live with uncertainty almost defines how you lead nowadays. Uncertainty may not suit everyone. For example, previous leaders relied heavily on techniques and plans to guide their thinking and behaviour. While logical steps and so-called rational thinking are desirable, they can be of limited value outside a stable context. In the twenty-first century the context will be anything but steady.

Naturally there will always remain some stable areas and these may require more traditional forms of leadership and management. These include areas such as health and safety, regulation, execution and logistics. Here it is still possible to rely on past practices and proven methods. All organisations need boundaries and due diligence – it's not a free-for-all.

However, in this book we do not focus on these unchanging or relatively static areas. Instead, we show the implications of the new, far more dynamic context. It's a world of irrationality and paradox, a source of both destructiveness and creativity. In this perplexing environment, relying on values, collaboration and talent will be more important than the top-down setting of goals to determine organisational direction. Leadership may spring from anywhere to determine goals. This may send shivers down the spines of traditionalists. Yet there have already been many organisations that have functioned almost entirely without the conventional authoritarian leader.

Given this constant sense of uncertainty there is, so far, no consensus on how you lead in such circumstances. But that has always been true of new forms of leadership. Our present description of how you go about it stems from practical encounters with those who are already *leading the way*. You can feel encouraged that many of the most successful, growing and sustainable organisations are being led right now by such new-style leaders.

Leadership is relational

At its simplest, *leading the way* means you make things happen with other people's support. That is, your leadership is relational. You may be able to lead yourself on your own, but to deliver outstanding results in the current situation you will need to engage and work with others. You need to work within the existing organisation structure and culture to generate new approaches, values, attitudes, behaviours and ideologies. In such an environment there is less clarity between who is leading and who is following.

In this book we will not be speaking of followers, or even subordinates. Those days are gone. In the new era, people will be leading colleagues, peers, stakeholders and supporters. This view of leading is only just beginning to penetrate the majority of today's organisations.[2] But it will almost certainly be extremely important in how future companies in the twenty-first century operate.

Leadership style

- **Task-oriented leader**. You care less about catering to employees, and are more concerned with finding technical, step-by-step solutions for meeting specific goals.
  You might ask 'What steps can we take to meet our quarterly financial goals?' as opposed to 'How can we build the kind of employee productivity that brings about success within the company?'
- **Relationship-oriented leader**. You understand the importance of tasks, but also place a tremendous amount of time and focus on meeting the needs of everyone involved in the assignment. This may involve:

[2] See, for example, Mary Uhl-Bien, *Relational Leadership Theory: Exploring the Social Processes of Leadership and Organizing*, University of Nebraska-Lincoln, 2006.

- creating engagement
- finding ways to inspire
- providing incentives, like bonuses or new work opportunities
- mediating to deal with workplace conflicts
- spending individual time with employees to learn their strengths and weaknesses
- offering above-average financial compensation, or just leading in a personable or encouraging manner.

Many organisations still rely heavily on task-oriented leaders. There are certainly benefits to this type of leadership. If you are a task-oriented leader, for example, your focus will be highly logical and analytical, and you will have a strong understanding of how to get the job done through workplace procedures. You also see a major task as involving numerous smaller tasks and delegate work accordingly. This way you ensure everything gets done in a timely and productive manner.

Similarly there are benefits in being a relationship-oriented leader. For you, productivity is paramount in meeting goals and succeeding, whether in a business environment or otherwise. Yet you also realise that building productivity requires a positive environment in which individuals do not feel driven. Personal conflicts, dissatisfaction with a job, resentment and even boredom can adversely affect productivity. So as a relationship-oriented leader you put people first to ensure that such problems stay at a minimum.

Probably no leader is entirely one or the other: task-driven or relationship-driven. However, there is a major shift under way towards the latter style, in which relationships count more in making things happen and in achieving personal and organisational success. This involves using values to drive performance, creating engagement, inspiring people, networking, generating constant innovation, managing risk and feeling comfortable with paradox. All these place considerable strain on the old-style employer/employee relationship, which relies so heavily on power structures and hierarchies.

How do you lead?

Leadership raises tricky issues, such as:

- What is your leadership style?
- Do you know how to lead diverse teams over which you have only limited authority?
- Are you able to create a fertile ground for fresh thinking and new ideas?
- Can you win people's loyalty, when perhaps the loudest unspoken question in the room is 'Why should anyone be led by you?'[3]
- Is your approach inclusive of people and diverse points of view – can you share ideas rather than selling or telling?
- Is what you are doing ethical?
- Do you follow a higher purpose?

Leading now is less about the pure mechanics – how you get people to do what you want – and more the tough task of finding common ground with people and building powerful relationships between them and you. It is no longer what you do but how you do it that is important: letting both the mind and the heart guide your way. Previous personal experience alone does not guarantee success.

[3] Rob Goffee and Gareth Jones, *Why Should Anyone Be Led By You?*, Harvard Business School Press, 2006.

Trouble at the top

Hugely experienced people sometimes lack relationship skills:

- **Carly Fiorina**, one of the most powerful women in corporate America, was forced out of the troubled computer maker by the company's board in 2005. Apart from not leading the company to renewed success, it was felt that she created considerable internal tension and conflict.
- Enron's **Jeffrey Skilling** was unquestionably clever and creative. Yet his misdirected and unprincipled approach to business was ultimately criminal. He seemed to lose his moral compass the more he became isolated from the humanising relationships with colleagues.
- When **Jack Griffin**, CEO of Time Inc., lost his job in 2011 after only five months, Time Warner explained that his 'leadership style and approach did not mesh with the company's'. Insiders called it a 'polarizing management style' and said that 'a good leader makes decisions that are inclusive, inspiring, motivating. With Jack, it was a demoralized, estranged group of execs.'[4]

Research has shown that high-level leaders are a curious mix, being modest yet wilful, humble yet fearless. Thus they tend to be both emotionally and socially intelligent. This allows them to value relationships and have a willingness to invest in developing them. Sometimes this is at the expense of the more mechanistic aspects of past leadership, such as corporate strategy, structures and bureaucratic processes.

To sum up, sustainable leadership is likely to involve more emphasis on relationships than pure tasks. Some experts call this new focus a 'post-industrial model of leadership', which is merely

[4] Jennifer Saba, 'Time Inc. CEO Jack Griffin ousted', Reuters, 18 February 2011.

a handy way of reminding you that you need to look afresh at what capabilities you will need to lead in the future. Putting it slightly differently, you will need to be concerned with the dynamics of how your relationships form and evolve in the workplace.

Leadership starts here!

Leading the way relies on a blend of personal behaviour, attitude and actions. These rest on two **foundations** which are the starting point for successful leadership in the twenty-first century: individuality and insight. No leader, in our view, will succeed in the coming years without paying considerable attention to, and investing in, developing both of these capabilities:

- **Individuality**: being yourself, having a distinctive style, driven by values, demonstrating integrity and character.
- **Insight**: self-awareness, understanding others and seeing the situation with clarity, often in new or unexpected ways.

Like all foundations, these two pillars of leadership are the building blocks supporting further action.

We also identify five **core capabilities** that leaders need to add value and make a difference:

- initiate
- involve
- inspire
- improvise
- implement.

As you may have noticed, all the skills conveniently begin with the letter I – which also reflects the personal and individual nature of leadership.

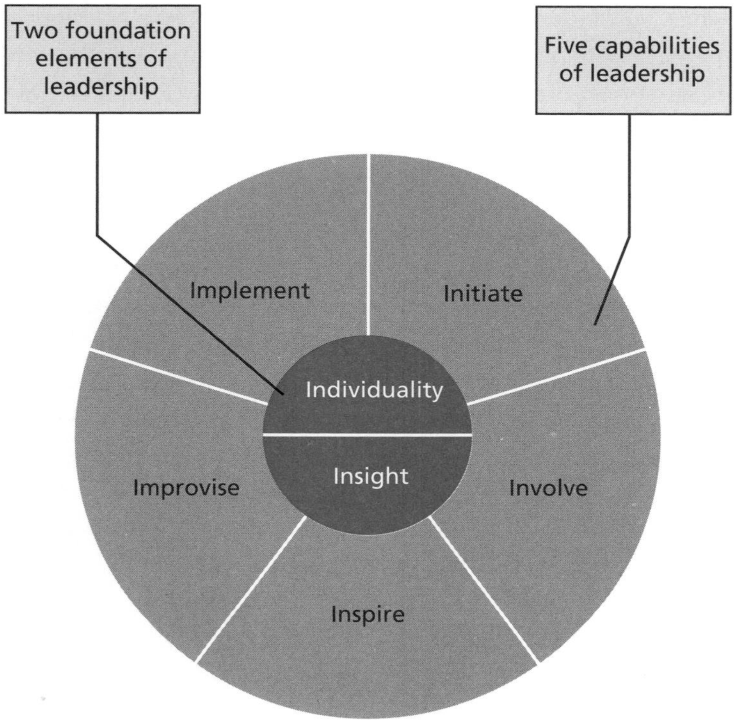

Together, the seven Is depict the journey you, as a leader, will undertake in order to produce change. It starts with who you are – your **individuality** defines the areas that you are interested in. These will be affected by your values, cares and concerns. You will then need **insight** in order to see what's needed around you. The effective use of insight will highlight what needs changing and where you need to focus your efforts. Thus the two foundation elements are where you start.

Then it is a question of employing the other five capabilities to ensure you are successful. So, you will decide what change you want to **initiate**. You will need to **involve** others in the scheme and **inspire** these stakeholders to engage in the project. However, once other people are involved, with their own opinions, talents and agendas, you will need to be flexible and creative in order to progress. This is where the ability to **improvise** becomes so crucial.

Plans change, other factors intrude, and the unforeseen happens. You will need to improvise new solutions to meet the ever-changing challenges and obstacles. Finally you **implement** with perseverance and resilience until you deliver results. Thus all seven leadership aptitudes are employed.

The two foundations can certainly be nourished and enhanced, yet not prescribed. And the core capabilities are entirely learnable. Thus you can acquire and develop these skills with sufficient practice and commitment. In the rest of this book we will show what this requires. For example, we suggest how leaders can be excellent at execution; that is, able to see through and implement changes both strategic and tactical. Similarly, we suggest that part of being an effective leader in this new era requires the ability to inspire people, and we suggest practical ways you can go about developing this important muscle.

We start with individuality because there is something intensely personal about leadership, even if leaders themselves modestly refrain from discussing themselves or their talents. You must decide for yourself which aspects of being a leader you need to develop and which you are already good at. Feedback, coaching and other forms of personal development can all shed light on how your leadership needs to change and grow.

In this book we offer guidance on what it will take to succeed in leadership. Ultimately, however, it is you – the 'I' of leadership – who decides whether you will step into this new style of leadership, and you who chooses whether to invest in your personal growth and development.

Few leaders get it right first time. Learning anything requires the willingness to experiment and get feedback. You learn to lead by constantly trying and sometimes failing. Every experience of leading offers lessons for improvement. If you are willing to keep learning and constantly practise, you are on the way to becoming the leader you aspire to be.

Your personal leadership mission needs to uncover what works for you as a leader. Never assume that because some other leader has found a way to make things happen, this is also your way. Only through practice will you come to lead instinctively, and practice means being willing to risk failure and even rejection.

> "I believe we learn by practice. Whether it means to learn to dance by practising dancing, or to learn to live by practising living, the principles are the same."
>
> **Martha Graham, dancer and teacher**

TWITTER SUMMARY

The world is changing and approaches to leadership must keep up. It needs a new approach involving seven essential skills.

RECAP

Global trends in the twenty-first century are altering expectations about what successful leaders must do to survive and thrive. New-style leaders must be able to live with continuing uncertainty and be good at building relationships. Their success will rely on the foundations of insight and individuality. Together with five additional capabilities, these add up to the seven Is of leadership in the twenty-first century.

01

Individuality

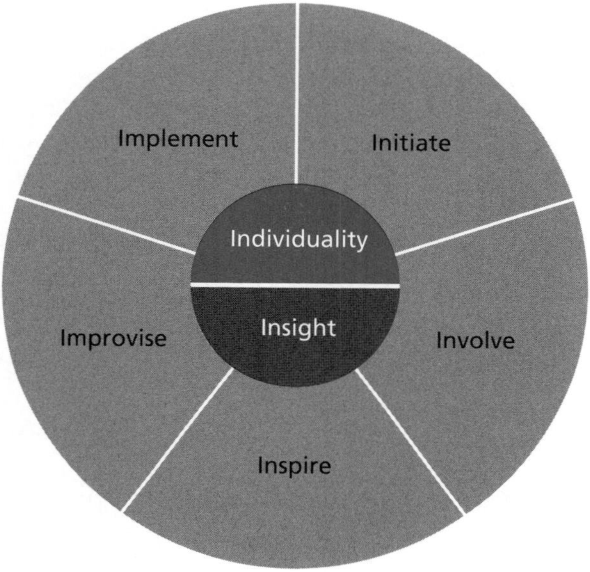

When Vineet Nayar became CEO of the $2.3 billion HCL Technologies he wondered how to show his 54,000 professionals in 26 countries that he was not a genius or a distant, godlike figure. His solution demonstrated his **individuality** in no uncertain terms. He called meetings around the world of about 4,000 people at a time. Before even making his opening remarks, he descended into the auditorium where people were sitting and began dancing to bouncy, catchy music. Soon he had everyone up and dancing.

After several minutes Nayar returned to the stage and, still panting from exertion, introduced himself. With a wry smile he explained that as everyone could see, he was not much of a dancer! You couldn't miss the message that this was someone who was not going to be governed by traditional, hierarchical methods. In his own words:

> Most CEO's are not as great as they're believed to be. There are exceptions. There is Bill Gates. There is Steve Jobs. There is Larry Page. But I'm not one of them, and so many of us are not them. So, if you see your job not

> as chief strategy officer and the guy who has all the ideas, but rather the guy who is obsessed with enabling employees to create value, I think you will succeed. That's a leadership style that evolved from my own understanding of the fact that I'm not the greatest and brightest leader born. My job is to make sure everybody is enabled to do what they do well.[1]

When you step into leadership, you bring your own individuality to the role. This is no ego trip. You simply realise how important it is for your colleagues to see you as willing to be yourself, and even revel in your distinctiveness. As part of this search for individuality, paradoxically you will also try hard to show you are one of them.

"Always remember you are absolutely unique – just like everyone else."

Margaret Mead, cultural anthropologist

We are all different, and really good leaders value that diversity throughout the organisation. As you take on more responsibility you will fully grasp the importance of nurturing individualism, both for yourself and of those around you.

The genius syndrome

A popular view of leadership is the genius syndrome. This is where you see your role as not merely highly individual, but as a 'genius with a thousand helpers'. In this increasingly questionable approach, you as leader explain a compelling personal vision and then enlist a crew of highly capable helpers. Your helpers accept almost any form of treatment, including coercion, in the cause of bringing your vaunted vision to life.

[1] Quoted from: Adam Bryant, 'He's not Bill Gates, or Fred Astaire', *New York Times*, 13 February 2010.

The trouble with this extreme form of narcissistic leadership is that it tends to fall apart once the so-called genius leaves. There are many examples of companies inextricably linked with a single, highly talented individual, whose future becomes questionable when they depart. Most recently the world wonders whether Apple can ever be as successful again without Steve Jobs at the helm. Similarly, in the UK, Richard Branson is Virgin, Philip Green is Arcadia. In listed companies, Rupert Murdoch (at the time of writing) is News Corporation and Anita Roddick was The Body Shop. But once these genius leaders go, how resilient is the company they leave behind?

After all, what greater testament is there to your greatness than if the place falls apart once you depart? This is leadership individuality gone mad. 'Companies want to be leader-proof. They don't want the companies to fall apart if the leader gets run over by a bus. But they do want to have the brand and charisma that comes with strong and detailed leadership,' says Nigel Nicholson, professor of organisational behaviour at the London Business School.[2]

It is quite possible to be an individual without being a power-mad, dictatorial egomaniac. You can nourish your individuality through your actions, attitudes and commitment to doing things in a distinctive way. The human mind is much affected by other minds. We tend to think what others think; and create along the lines others have created. But our individuality allows us to break out of this mode; to think differently and manifest what has not existed before. In fact, individuality is to think and create something out of nothing – it is the essence of creativity.

[2] BBC News, 'Does Apple's Jobs mean companies can be one-man bands?', 18 January 2011.

"You have your way. I have my way. As for the right way, the correct way, and the only way, it does not exist."

Friedrich Nietzsche, philosopher

Research into outstanding leaders confirms their intense individualism. This tendency or capability seems set to play an even greater role in twenty-first-century organisations. With their need for constant innovation, permanent performance improvement, high levels of engagement and an ability to adapt quickly to a changing environment, we can expect leaders of these organisations to look for distinctive, rather than one-size-fits-all solutions.

What price charisma?

In our early work on leadership we, like many others, assumed all successful leaders must be overflowing with charisma. That is, you must be the sort of person who makes an instant and huge impression on people. Your entry into a room, for example, would always become an 'event'.

By charisma we mean the ability to use your entire self to make a usually positive personal impact on people and, through them, on the organisation as a whole. When people talk about inspirational leaders they mainly mean those with a powerful charisma. We see it in some of the publicity-seeking individuals mentioned earlier.

Yet despite its high profile in ideas about what makes a successful leader, charisma turns out to be far less important than once thought. The seminal work of Jim Collins in *Good to Great,* for example, showed convincingly that while some leaders are naturally endowed with enviable talents, and occasionally remarkable charisma, this is not nearly as critical to running a successful organisation as previously thought. We see no reason why this conclusion should significantly alter in the coming years.

> "Charisma becomes the undoing of leaders, making them inflexible and convinced of their own infallibility and unable to change."
>
> **Peter Drucker, influential writer and management consultant**

What conclusions do we draw from this for you, as you take the lead? Mainly that you do not necessarily need to brim over with colourful charisma, useful though that may be. It can be enough to be full of character and distinctiveness.

The source of individuality

There is an exercise that we regularly run on our leadership workshops where we ask participants to reflect on their journey into leadership. We ask participants to identify what have been the experiences that have shaped them as a leader. Who has influenced them? What have they learnt from the various incidents that have propelled them into taking on the mantle of leadership in the way that they currently do?

Invariably, people will talk of role models, of inherited family characteristics, and often people such as teachers or coaches who have believed in them and encouraged their growth. All these factors will influence your personal style and approach.

Combined with your values and integrity, they will also contribute to your distinctive character and individuality. Let us have a look at some of these factors in more detail.

Being yourself

Dianne Thompson, a butcher's daughter from Batley, became Camelot's chief executive and defeated the more high-profile Richard Branson's bid to run the lottery. Battling to get the company back in the race for a renewed lottery licence, she was, said non-executive director Michael Grade, 'just herself. There was no PR spin. She believed in the cause, she was a master of the facts and the detail ... she came over as a real person.'

It can be hard to be yourself when pressures all around try to make you into someone else. Simply fitting in can mean sacrificing some of your important distinctive qualities – from frankness to integrity, from sensitivity to humour. Pressures to conform can be enervating. For example, the highly successful operations director of a well-known UK food concern was being groomed to become managing director. He was warned discreetly that he needed to stop being so ready to say what he thought. To satisfy the City he should start wearing suits. A close colleague said, with sadness, 'I could just see him slowly becoming a grey person. It's like I could see one arm turning grey while the rest of him was still special; soon, maybe, the rest would follow.'

To be truly yourself is first to be authentic and second to possess considerable self-knowledge. Most people need to work at both of these.

Authenticity is not so much a skill as a willingness to be selectively vulnerable, to show people who you are. Many commentators have remarked that President Obama appears to be a man who is comfortable in his own skin. He writes movingly in his memoir, *Dreams from My Father*, about his experiences growing up with a white mother and a black father in America and Indonesia. It caused him to reflect deeply on his identity and helped him to develop his authenticity.

Depending on how you go about it, if you show your vulnerability to people they will tend to see it not as weakness but as authenticity. They are likely to respond to your leadership, not with disdain but respect, not with disgust but empathy. If you are fearful of showing your humanity you merely emphasise your lack of self-confidence. Instead of appearing human, you will come across as overconfident and a know-it-all. This breeds neither loyalty nor respect.

Self-knowledge is a life-time's journey and most successful leaders, now and in the future, will always be on that path. It involves several actions coming together: you are you own best teacher; you accept responsibility without blaming others; you realise you can learn anything you want to learn; you reflect on your experiences; and you accept yourself with all your strengths and weaknesses. In short, it's about being true to yourself.

"To be yourself in a world that is constantly trying to make you something else is the greatest accomplishment."

Ralph Waldo Emerson, essayist, lecturer and poet

When you accept who you are, you can admire other people without trying to be them. Because the boss walks around in sweaters and jeans, for example, does not mean you must do the same.

Being grounded in your sense of identity allows you to tackle issues with a confidence that may have a profound effect on others. Who you are defines what you want to achieve. A strong sense of personal identity also helps you to come across as authentic. That is, you are someone who speaks from the heart. So an important part of building a clear identity is your ability to articulate and share what really matters to you – that is, expressing your values.

There is no short cut to achieving a strong personal identity. It's a journey of many years and you are already on it. Yet this journey is not a passive one in which you drift along hoping your identity will build by itself. Instead you can choose to:

- stay aware of your journey of discovery
- seek experiences that test and strengthen your identity.

Research in the field of positive psychology suggests that living life in a conscious and mindful way gives you a distinct advantage in a number of fields of endeavour. By strengthening your sense of self, you become more able to harness your talents and apply them in order to affect the world around you.

"The foundation of leadership is not thinking, behaviour, competencies, techniques, or position. The foundation of leadership is who we are – our identify or foundational state."

Robert E. Quinn, Professor in Business Administration, University of Michigan Ross School of Business

Personal experience

Human beings learn and grow from their experiences. This is partly what makes you special and hones your leadership individuality. Personal experience only becomes a negative if you over-emphasise it at the expense of others, for example by downgrading the value of their own experiences. Sharing your personal experiences can be an important way to build strong relationships with colleagues and supporters. This is particularly true when it involves showing vulnerability, or your 'human side'.

Unfortunately, no organisation can commit enough time and resources to ensuring that you grow and develop fully. So you need to take charge of expanding your personal experience. It will always be your job to look for new opportunities to enlarge your horizons.

You probably bring a wealth of experience and personal history to your leadership role. Sometimes this may seem to have little connection with your actual employment. But often you have experience that can be very valuable. For example, mothers who juggle childcare and a job have a profound understanding of what it takes to be organised, solve problems, give direction and set boundaries.

We are our history, and yet we are also much more than our history. While past experience has value, in our fast-changing world it may prevent you taking a fresh look at what is happening around you. When *leading the way*, you need to get used to tackling each issue afresh, basing your ideas on the assumptions that:

- There is a solution out there, we just have to find it.
- This has to be worth solving or resolving, otherwise let's not waste time on it.

Using these two starting points you can direct your energy to approach each new situation with an enquiring mind, a readiness to do things differently. The best leaders readily abandon old ideas and in doing so provide an inspiration for others. When Alexander cut the Gordian knot, rather than trying to unravel it, he was not just cheating, he was refusing to let past experience dictate how he solved the problem. One of the things past experience teaches us is that the innovative solutions are not rooted in the past.

So, how do you go about capitalising on your personal experience? One of the simplest ways is always to conduct a debrief of every project, large or small. Dissect every failure, not to apportion blame, but to answer the simple question: 'What can we learn from this?'

Another way is to share your personal experiences with others and ask whether they have ones to share with you. Putting your combined experience to work may well produce an unexpected solution.

Personal style

"To live is not just to survive, but to thrive with passion, compassion, some humour and style."

Maya Angelou, author and poet

Reto Wittwer, CEO of Kempinski Hotels (the world's oldest luxury hotel group), has always done things his own way. 'There was never anybody I wanted to be like,' he says. 'I saw people and thought: "If I ever have an opportunity to get to this position, I will be significantly different".'[3]

Like Wittwer, the more you insist on being yourself, the more distinctive you will appear to other people. Uniqueness speaks for itself and helps you stand out from the crowd. Of course, there is no universal formula for being distinctive and expressing your individualism. Each leader does it differently. A good starting point is to ask: 'Am I prepared to value my distinctiveness?'

You can be distinctive by how you walk, talk, deal with people, listen, get things done, dress, solve problems and so on. Similarly, when you hit resistance to what you want to achieve, what is your reaction? Is it to slow down, back track, immediately to seek a compromise? How you handle differences can also serve to make you distinctive.

[3] Hotel Management-Network.com, 'Lessons in luxury', 8 October 2008.

"The thing that makes you exceptional is inevitably that which must also make you lonely."

Lorraine Hansberry, playwright and author

When you stamp your personal signature on what you do, in whatever form this takes, you will have a distinctive approach that other people immediately recognise. In marketing terms, you start to become a 'brand'. This may simply come down to a pattern of consistent and recognisable behaviour that sets you apart from others. The strongest part of your style may be something that you least recognise or even value. Perhaps it is your humour, your directness or your empathy that people find appealing about you as a leader. You may need feedback from others to help you see this. Only by knowing your personal assets can you capitalise on them.

Your strong personal style can also provide an opportunity to be the opposite of how you are normally seen, without losing yourself. It is a bit like an artist's palette. You have all sorts of colours available to you. An artist who uses only red and blue might like to explore some of the other colours to widen their range. The same goes for your self-expression. You have a colourful range of expression available to you that you can employ in different situations. This does not mean you will lose your own identity. For example, if you are generally pleasant and smiley this allows you plenty of room to occasionally be tough, challenging and uncompromising, without losing your natural warmth. Similarly, if you tend to be a rather serious, thoughtful person there will be scope to be exactly the opposite, without being immediately regarded as frivolous. The more variety you have in your expression, the more you can bring the appropriate responses to different situations.

Personal style also translates directly into your leadership style. This is how you approach giving direction, implementing plans and seeking people's engagement. Researchers have long identified different styles and named three major ones:

- **Authoritarian/autocratic.** You tell employees what you want done and how you want it accomplished without inviting their advice. This only really works if you have all the information to solve the problem, are short on time, and employees are well motivated. Some people tend to think of this style as a vehicle for yelling, using demeaning language, leading by threats and abusing their power. This is not an authoritarian style, rather it is an abusive, unprofessional style called 'bossing people around'. It has no place in a leader's repertoire and certainly does not describe the typical successful twenty-first-century approach.
- **Participative/democratic.** You focus on engaging and involving one or more employees in the decision-making process. You seek their help to decide what to do and how to do it. However, as leader you retain the final decision-making authority. To exercise your individuality through this style is not a sign of weakness but rather a sign of strength that your employees will respect. This style is normally used when you have part of the information and your employees have other parts. A leader is not expected to know everything – this is why you employ knowledgeable and skilful employees. Using this style is of mutual benefit – it allows employees to become part of the team and allows you to make better decisions.
- **Delegating and free rein.** You allow others to make the decisions. However, you continue to be responsible for the actual decisions. This style works best when employees can analyse the situation and determine what needs to be done and how to do it. You cannot do everything! You must set priorities and delegate certain tasks.

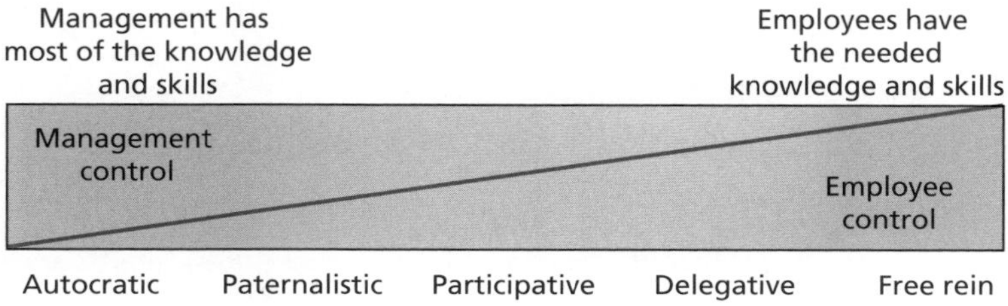

Leadership styles

Each of the various styles assumes different levels of knowledge and skills of those involved. So at one end of a spectrum leaders have total management control, while at the other end employees do.

You will probably use a combination of all these styles, depending on what forces are involved between you, your stakeholders and the situation. For example, you might use an authoritarian style with a new employee who is just learning the job – you may be directive and show clearly what needs to be done. You might use a participative style with a team of workers who know their job – who know about a problem but do not have all the information. Finally, you might use a delegating style with someone who knows more about the job than you. You cannot do everything and other employees need to take ownership of their jobs.

Your awareness of these different styles is what matters more than any attempt to pick a particular style. Your style should be most influenced by the situation you face. Factors that influence your approach will include the answers to the following questions:

- How much time is available?
- Are relationships based on respect and trust and not disrespect?
- Who has the information – you, your colleagues, or both?
- How well are your team trained and how well do you know the task?

- Are there any internal conflicts?
- What are stress levels like?
- What is the type of task: is it structured, unstructured, complicated or simple?
- Are there any relevant laws, established procedures, health and safety regulations or development plans?

To be a forward-thinking leader you will need to search for the appropriate approach and style. It might help to visit colleagues in other organisations, use outside consultants, accept personal coaching, conduct 360-degree feedback studies and adopt any other ways to give you a useful perspective on leadership and an accurate view of how you are seen by others.

Personal values

"We cannot be sure that we have something worth living for, unless we are ready to die for it."

Eric Hoffer, social writer

During the Nazi occupation of his country in the Second World War, King Christian X of Denmark noticed a Nazi flag flying over a Danish public building. He immediately called the German commandant, demanding that the flag be taken down at once. The commandant refused. 'Then a soldier will go and take it down,' said the king. 'He will be shot,' threatened the commandant. 'I think not,' replied the king, 'for I shall be the soldier.' Within minutes the flag was taken down. The king was courageous, showed leadership and prevailed.

Values will matter a great deal in successful twenty-first-century organisations. This is because such organisations will depend on their people, rather than capital investment, as their main resource for staying competitive and encouraging constant innovation. Values matter because they help shape your behaviour and it is behaviour that influences other people.

People can be categorised into several generations, for example Gen Y, Gen X and so on. Each has its own special motivation needs. As a leader you need to understand people, whatever their age. You need to uncover their skills, strengths and whatever motivates them. In short, you have to recognise that everyone is different and deal with each employee as an individual.[4]

There is nothing esoteric about values and how they can guide you as a leader. They are simply what you care passionately about and what you value most. What matters to you? You will find the answers in your work, your possessions and your relationships. Try reviewing all three as you answer the following questions:

- Can you identify the values that really matter?
- Are these of any use to other people?
- Are your values mainly positive or negative in their outlook? (Destructive values, for example, will seldom win widespread support.)

> "The trouble with the rat race is that even if you win, you are still a rat."
>
> **Lily Tomlin, actress, writer and producer**

Could you explain your personal values to other people? Everybody knows what Ghandi stood for, less so for leaders such as President Bush Snr.

[4] See, for example, Léo F. C. Bruno and Eduardo G. E. Lay, 'Personal values and leadership effectiveness', *Journal of Business Research*, **16** (6), 2008.

Making sense of your values

- Write out your personal credo or what really matters to you.
- Spend time clarifying these values – what do they really mean in practice?
- Review the behavioural implications of each value – how would anyone notice them?
- Make your values visible to others by behaving consistently with them.
- What evidence is there of you living your values?
- Talk about them to others – why they matter to you.
- Invite people to comment on your values.

Finally, having strong values will allow you to bounce back after setbacks. Because you know what you stand for, you are unlikely to be deterred or undermined by failure. Challenges are there to test your resolve and what you stand for. Setbacks are opportunities to show your character and resilience.

Though personal values may sound a vague concept, people soon understand what you mean when you articulate your values and live by them through your actions. When you engage in a dialogue about values, people develop a sense of their own and others' positions.

The dialogue you provoke might be about how you value stakeholders, how to make your workplace a great place to be, how best to satisfy certain customers, and so on. Talking openly about values brings them alive and will fill your people with energy and enthusiasm.

Integrity

Comedian Groucho Marx joked: 'I have principles and if you don't like them, I have others!' The new generation of leaders sees it differently. You can express your individuality through strong personal values and, if you live by them, you will manifest integrity.

In numerous studies of managers, integrity shows up as the single characteristic most often mentioned as essential for leadership. That is, someone who is truthful, trustworthy, of sound character and strong convictions. Sadly such integrity is sometimes missing: studies show that misconduct in organisations remains high and it is often serious. Lack of integrity is often driven by work pressures, inadequate resources and job uncertainties.[5]

Looking to the future, there are many reasons to conclude that successful leaders will be those with a strong moral compass and an ability to turn integrity from an abstract concept into practical action that guides and inspires the organisation. Successful organisations need to avoid reputational damage, the cost of fraud and malpractices, loss of trust leading to poor performance and wasteful staff attrition, and so on. The leaders who emerge in the coming years are likely to be able to see the value of integrity as a strong corporate asset. They will be acutely aware of the truth in Warren Buffet's assertion that 'It takes 20 years to build a reputation and five minutes to ruin it. If you think about that, you'll do things differently.'

'Babe' Zaharias was a champion in the 1932 Olympics and later a successful professional golfer. On one occasion she penalised herself two strokes when she accidentally played the wrong ball. 'Why did you do it?' asked a friend. 'No one saw you; no one would have known the difference.' 'I would have known,' Zaharias replied.

[5] See, for example, KPMG, *Integrity Survey 2008–2009*.

It is possible to survive a long time without showing much integrity. The notorious Bernard Madoff, for example, managed to survive for years, but his deceit and duplicity eventually caught up with him. Leaders without integrity are usually destructive and untrustworthy, and not what we are talking about in this book. Leaders with integrity have personal values running through their whole being like a gold seam.

Integrity is not about profit, or even about whether you have the right to do something under the law. Integrity is about doing the right thing. It explains and confirms that famous aphorism that 'Managers do it right, leaders do what is right'. Company scandals, such as Enron, Andersen, WorldCom, Union Carbide, Fannie Mae, Royal Bank of Scotland and so on, have merely highlighted the importance of having leaders with a personal commitment to integrity.

"Integrity is the essence of everything successful."

Richard Buckminster Fuller, architect, engineer, author, inventor and futurist

Integrity in action

- Character over personal gain.
- People over things.
- Service over power.
- Discipline over impulse.
- Mission over convenience.
- The long view over the immediate.

You can demonstrate your integrity in highly practical and high-profile ways. For example, you uphold agreements, honour contracts, keep your word, tell the truth, say what you mean and mean what you say. Thus you become an integrated human being where your outward expression is consistent with your thinking and feeling. You will have integrated all the aspects of you into a coherent and consistent self. Consequently you are likely to be thought of with affection, pride and sometimes with envy.

Integrity barometer

Not everyone is willing to do what it takes to behave with integrity in practice. Try answering these five questions about your next important decision or choice of action:

- Am I willing to say what I think and risk being wrong?
- Does this conduct make me a better person?
- Would I want someone I love to do that?
- Am I leading by example and taking 100 per cent responsibility?
- Do I tackle crises with integrity?

Apart from answering these questions for yourself, you can also *lead the way* by pursuing integrity across the organisation. Here are some actions you might initiate or encourage others to pursue:

- Build integrity into the vision and values of the organisation.
- Make sure you and others are setting appropriate goals.
- Install high ethical standards into all processes and systems, with suitable controls.
- Search for and welcome the truth.
- Provide channels for reporting issues through openness, internal audits, etc.
- Include integrity into all senior managers' job descriptions.
- Make appraisals hold people to account for lapses in integrity.
- Benchmark practices internally and externally, using independent help to review governance.

- Conduct regular staff surveys on ethics and regular checks on how leaders are perceived.
- Ensure decision making is consistent with organisational values.

Taking a stand

Having a strong sense of self and knowing when to take a stand is an important part of leadership. It is often your responsibility to take courageous decisions. While leadership these days is, on the whole, a collaborative endeavour, there are times when you need enough self-belief to stand alone and be answerable for difficult choices.

Knowing what you stand for is part of your integrity. For example, Howard Schultz, CEO of Starbucks, took his stand when Starbucks was unsure whether to move into a particular international market. Schultz was advised against the move by every analysis he read. He spent over half a million dollars on consultants, who also told him not to go. All his direct reports were also opposed to the move. Schultz met again with his team, listened to their concerns, answered their questions and asked for their support. In the end, he mobilised his management team, went with his heart – with what he thought was right – and entered the market in question. Schultz stood his ground and, ultimately, was able to score another successful expansion of Starbucks into the international marketplace.

Networking

Leadership is about relationships. Therefore, tomorrow's successful leaders will express their individuality through being active networkers. Across all sectors, networking is already an essential and widely recognised aspect of leadership. Successful CEOs spend most of their time with other people, networking in one form or another.[6]

[6] See, for example, O. Bandieri, L. Guiso, A. Prat and R. Sadun, 'How do CEOs spend their time?' VoxEU.org, 28 May 2011.

The upsurge in social networking may seem rather remote from the leadership role and yet is another way to promote one's individuality. It can include having profiles, friends, blog posts, widgets, and perhaps something unique to a particular social networking website – such as the ability to 'poke' people on Facebook, or high-five someone on hi5, or join in LinkedIn discussion groups. Even total sceptics of such encounters find it can be useful, which partly explains why Rupert Murdoch started tweeting!

Networking in all its varied forms expands how you exercise leadership. For example, it can help you break down silos and foster collaboration and collective leadership. With the expected continued growth in connectivity, decline in hierarchies and increase in new creative forms of collaboration, networking will come to define your leadership – as someone who:

- builds relationships with allies
- creates a neutral space for diverse people to engage in dialogue and action
- uses culture and other differences to influence action.

An important part of being a leader therefore is your refusal to be isolated, and determination to draw on a diverse range of sources for support. For instance, you can make use of mentoring, interest groups, discussion forums, 'communities of practice' and peer learning. All these can feed you with information, stimuli and confidence to take relevant action.

Try asking yourself: 'How many people do I know whom I can personally trust to give me honest and helpful advice?' Networking can help you expand that number.

However, building networks that support your leadership will fail if you do it merely to extract business from people. Likewise, any attempt to manipulate people to advance your career will not succeed. As with any relationship, networking requires you constantly to work at it. You cannot ignore someone for years and then expect them to perform favours when you contact them out of the blue. Nurture your contacts and spend time looking after them.

If, as we believe, leadership is about finding where you can add value and then doing so, you can start by practising adding value to your contacts. Seek opportunities to help them out when you can. Pass on ideas or information if you feel it will support them.

The more you put out, the more you more will get back.

"The secret of success is consistency of purpose."

Benjamin Disraeli, statesman and author

TWITTER SUMMARY

It's you as a person and your ability to build relationships that are crucial to your success as a leader.

RECAP

Leadership individuality is a mixture of being yourself, personal experience, personal style, personal values, integrity and building networks.

IDEAS FOR ACTION

- ✔ Value your distinctiveness. It could be how you walk, talk, deal with people, get things done, make decisions, dress, communicate, define or solve problems, follow your convictions and so on.
- ✔ Seek experiences that test and strengthen your identity.
- ✔ Be willing to create a personal plan to develop yourself, even if you are already in a senior company position.

- ✔ Dissect every failure and success – not to apportion blame or credit, but to answer a simple question: 'What can I learn from this?'
- ✔ Study others who have already mastered the skills you need. What personal experiences will help you to become a master of them too?
- ✔ Explore both the good and the bad elements of your style. Only if you know and acknowledge the assets can you capitalise on them.
- ✔ Visit colleagues in different organisations, use outside consultants, and use a coach or mentor to gain a different perspective.
- ✔ Write out your personal credo of what matters to you. What do you really care about?
- ✔ Make values visible by behaving consistently with them. If you value quality, for instance, then it should appear in everything you do; if you value efficiency, then *lead the way* by being highly efficient yourself.
- ✔ Invent your own ways of focusing on values – making them explicit, sharing them, keeping them high profile and constantly talking about them.
- ✔ Encourage others to talk about values.
- ✔ Cherish your personal integrity by always doing what you say you'll do. This means you are consistent, keep to agreements, honour contracts and keep to your word.
- ✔ Use networking to break down silos and foster collaboration and collective leadership.
- ✔ Ask yourself how many people you know whom you can personally trust to give you honest and helpful advice.
- ✔ Nurture your contacts and spend time looking after them. Like any relationship, networking requires you constantly to work at it. Seek opportunities to help your contacts out and add value to them when you can.

02

Insight

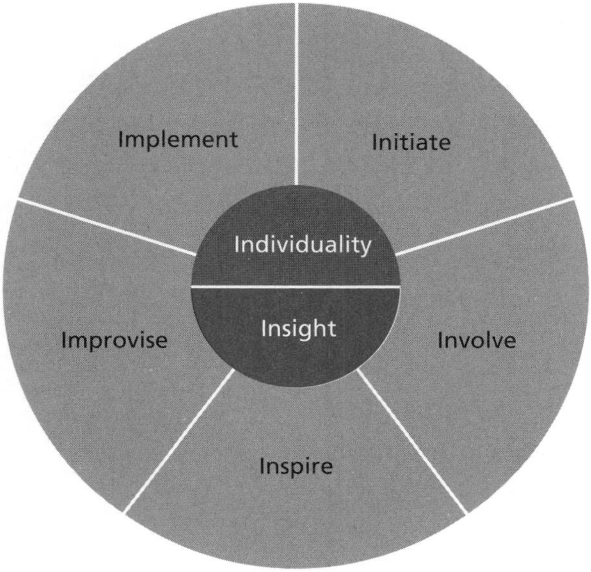

Do you sometimes see what others cannot? This is the essence of **insight** – your unique ability to make sense of disparate events, information and experiences. Using this facility, you arrive at a picture of the world that others may only come to see with your help. Broadly, you need to be concerned with the kind of insight that will help you understand yourself, the people you interact with and the environment and events that occur. You need to be able to see what's needed in the world around you and where to focus your attention.

Insight has long been recognised as a critical factor in creating personal and organisational success. An influential twentieth-century expert on organisations once observed that a company's competitive advantage 'will come from an historically underdeveloped asset: the ability to capture and apply insights from diverse fields'.[1]

This underdeveloped asset is now increasingly a focus of attention, as organisations face dizzying amounts of information from

[1] See, for example, A. Di Fiore, 'Strategic insight is not on the CEO radar', Harvard Business Review Blog Network, 25 January 2012.

countless sources, more complexity in their environment and ever-widening forms of competition and innovation. There is consequently a growing recognition of the importance of developing and using leadership insight to make sense of such challenges. To be frank, if you lack insight in the coming years, you will almost certainly find it hard to succeed as a leader.

This invaluable foundation ability to interpret the world around you can set you apart as a leader. It consists of three main areas:

- self-awareness
- understanding other people
- seeing what's going on.

Self-awareness

It was a terrible personal shock for Michael Mack when he was fired as CEO from the US restaurant group Garden Fresh he had helped to build. He had proved rather less than an inspirational leader. Instead, he acted more like a distant consultant, since that was his background. Despite his dismissal, miraculously Mack stayed close to his company while continuing to offer help, without showing any bitterness. Instead, he systematically developed a good relationship with his colleagues that had been previously missing. Three years later, in 1994, he was invited to return as a changed and far more open CEO.

Mack's increased self-awareness explains how he was able to use personal insight both about himself and what was going on inside his previous company. His method for increasing self-awareness included the use of outside advisers and various techniques like recording thoughts in a journal. He also learned how to balance work and family.[2]

[2] Alison Beard, 'Losing the top job – and winning it back', *Harvard Business Review*, October 2010.

"I think self-awareness is probably the most important thing towards being a champion."

Billie Jean King, tennis champion

Self-awareness occurs when you notice how you typically behave, or are perceived by others. There are many ways to expand this awareness, but they must all begin with a commitment to invest serious time in this aspect of your growth. Practical ways to sharpen your self-awareness include:

- **Self-insight**. This depends on the work you do on your personal growth and development. A somewhat hazy concept, self-insight is really about recognising personal strengths and weaknesses, and being conscious of how you are at any moment. It includes knowing when your personal assets, such as persistence or determination, are being overused, and realising when these can turn into liabilities, such as intransigence or intolerance.[3]
- **Self-assessment**. Leadership development programmes often encourage self-assessment by asking participants to evaluate themselves and the impact they make. For instance, you may complete a personality measure or a rating form asking you to evaluate your performance and behaviours. You may get comparative information from similar ratings made by your senior manager, peers, or line-reports (see page 194).
- **Feedback**. The best leaders are endlessly curious to know what effect they are having on people. Your sources of feedback may include developmental assessment centres, 360-degree or upward feedback, performance appraisals from managers, regular reports such as weekly sales reports, and visits to different locations within the organisation.

[3] See, for example, Manuel London, *Leadership Development: Paths to Self-Insight and Professional Growth*, Psychology Press, 2001.

- **Coaching**. This is an increasingly popular way of growing your self-awareness. External consultants who coach executives usually have a background in business, human resources, performance facilitation, management or psychology. Their role is to help you process feedback and use it to set development goals.
- **Group facilitation**. You can learn a great deal about yourself by systematically setting out to observe your performance in group settings. You can discover how people receive your communications and sometimes don't, despite your best intentions. Some groups hire facilitators to help the group do its work. The facilitator or workshop leader focuses on the group process, for instance the clarity of communication and the extent to which all members have a chance to participate. The facilitator may also stop the group's work occasionally to elicit discussion of the group process so members can examine how they work together.
- **Role-playing exercises and simulations**. You might attend a leadership development workshop that uses various challenging experiences to help participants become more aware of their strengths and weaknesses. These exercises allow you to test and rehearse new behaviours in a relatively non-threatening setting. Methods might include role-reversals, placing you in a new setting, and forcing recognition of roles and relationships. For instance, you might be asked to take the role of someone else in your team and, in the process, may see job demands and stresses and their own behaviour from a different perspective.

These are just some of the practical ways you can interpret and indeed develop self-awareness. Only by accurately seeing how you are processing and responding to the world around you can you then set about transforming it.

"Nothing is more terrible than activity without insight."

Thomas Carlyle, essayist and historian

Who you are is how you lead. This is why leadership is autobiographical. Many people spend a lot of time focusing externally and yet miss the thing closest to them – their inner world. Insight into your inner world reveals the forces that govern and influence so much of what you do in life. Understanding yourself better can help to explain why things are working or not. And this understanding enables you to apply yourself more efficiently. The better you know yourself, the more you become clear about:

- Who are you?
- What is driving you?
- When are you at your best and why?
- What impact do you have on people?
- How do you need to change?
- What difference can you make?
- How do you respond to conflict?
- What's your point of view?
- How and where do you add value?
- What's the point of you?

You do not necessarily need to share this self-knowledge with anyone. However, an increasing number of leaders in search of greater self-awareness find one-to-one coaching a useful way of acquiring fresh insight into themselves and, equally important, the effect they have on others. Attention by researchers, particularly the work of Daniel Goleman on self-awareness, shows clearly what this means in practice. Goleman, for example, offers plenty of scientific data confirming the importance of emotional intelligence and self-awareness in leadership.

Becoming more self-aware is not as mystical as it sounds. It is simply knowing how you see yourself, understanding your personality and its impact – its strengths and weaknesses – and clarifying your purpose. Self-aware leaders are no mere navel-gazers. They are simply willing to make enough time to reflect on what is going on inside them and how this may be affecting others and the situation.

Incidentally, as we indicate later in Chapter 6, in the section on presence, self-awareness is not the same as being self-conscious. In the latter you stay so focused on yourself you can hardly absorb anything that is not solely about you. Putting it slightly differently, being self-conscious is all about me, me, me. Being self-aware is about me *and* you.

Personal enquiry

Have you ever experienced arriving somewhere without actively thinking about the route or what kind of driving you used to get there? Suddenly you 'come to' and realise where you are. Many people live their lives like that – as if on autopilot. They go through the motions in an automatic way until suddenly something occurs to awaken them and they realise they have not been in control of their lives. They realise they have not been making conscious decisions.

Leadership demands attention – a willingness to continually question yourself about feelings, motivations and behaviour. To develop a clearer picture of your own strengths and areas for development, try creating a personal balance sheet. Even writing down such a list can be a useful start; you need never show it to anyone else.

Psychometric tests or personality profiles are another route to gaining a fresh perspective on the 'real you'. For example, they can help clarify your preferred role in a team, highlight your tendency to take instant action or spend too long reflecting, show whether you care more about people than things, confirm whether you are introspective or an extrovert, reveal how you prefer to learn, and so on.

> "What lies behind us and what lies in front of us are tiny matters compared to what lies within us."
>
> **Ralph Waldo Emerson, essayist, lecturer and poet**

Internal cast

To portray a range of characters accurately, experienced actors learn to access different parts of themselves. These sub-personalities are like an internal cast of characters, a databank on which they can draw to portray other people truthfully.

You, too, have an internal cast of characters. You possess a rich inner world, such as the enthusiast, the achiever, the bully, the pleaser, the coward, the lover, the joker, the procrastinator, the music lover, the eccentric, the worrier, the critic, the peace-maker, and so on. Do you recognise any of these?

If something inside you seems to say 'But I don't have an internal cast of characters', you have just heard from one! Who is it – the sceptic, the anxious adult, the fearful child?

This internal cast influences how you behave and respond to the world. If you are to *lead the way* then you will need to recognise the existence of this rich internal resource and use it to achieve an impact. Like an actor, you mobilise it to affect others and to guide you in how to perform in different situations.

Explore your internal cast of characters

1 Start by listing some recent difficult or memorable situations you have encountered.

2 Try to recall in detail how you responded – got angry, felt bored, gave up, laughed, left the room, argued stridently, retreated into passivity, and so on.

▶

3 Identify an internal character who seems to keep popping up, influencing how you behave.

4 Now review:

- When does this character seem to take over?
- What seems to trigger this character's arrival?
- What control do you have over this character?
- What influence does this internal character have on your leadership?
- Does this character get in the way or help?

5 Having identified a character, decide whether it helps or hinders you in a leadership role.

6 Consider ways in which you might get this character more under your conscious control.

Understanding other people

For some years at Maynard Leigh we used to have a 'feelings' white board on the wall. It was in response to our team's growing awareness of how people's emotions affect everyone's mood and performance. So, each morning team members would arrive and add a face and a word to describe their feelings. If someone drew a frown and added the word 'grumpy' you knew it was a good idea to give them some space. An upset face might engender enquiries as to their well-being. Seeing a word like 'powerful' might mean it was time to engage that person's energies.

Perhaps it's an unfair generalisation, but the average manager often knows more about the computer on their desk than about the people they are supposed to manage and lead. In the absence of knowledge, the tendency is to be judgemental.

That is, you resort to making assumptions about people. This includes stereotyping them and not seeing beyond the surface. Or you develop blind spots and simply miss the potential in those you lead.

In contrast, good leaders are curious and really want to understand how other people tick. They are socially intelligent – that is, they empathise with others, imagining what it is like to be in their shoes. Instead of leaping to conclusions or making assumptions about people, you need to observe their behaviour, engage them in conversation, ask questions and really listen.

Your impact when using insight in this way can be surprising to those on the receiving end. For example, people may say things like:

- How did she know I felt that way?
- He said exactly what I was thinking.
- She really got my point.
- He really listens to you.

You can achieve this kind of effect by paying close attention and using insightful analysis. Naturally it is a lifetime's work building an ability to understand others, which is why you will need to keep trying to grasp what drives your colleagues.

One of the best ways of really understanding other people is by separating out three processes that take place in our minds when we see them. As soon as information enters your brain, you start an instant process of interpretation. This process of perception happens so fast that you sometimes forget that you may not be seeing accurately. And the human mind will often then take you straight into wondering or imagining things about people.

On the workshops we run, we help participants separate out fact from interpretation by using an exercise called:

- observe
- perceive
- wonder.

By continually challenging your assumptions about people you can start seeing them afresh. And it all starts with observation. This is deliberate people-watching – consciously observing them in all kinds of different situations, seeing how they behave. You cannot stay distant, acting like a puppet master pulling other people's strings. Instead the focus of the observation is information – anything that is factually true about them.

Having observed accurately, you can then start the interpretation process and notice your perceptions about people. They may seem angry, pleasant, troubled, weird, pre-occupied, upset, in a hurry, etc. Perception thus becomes a conscious process where you notice your own judgements and interpretations of people's actions. And you know that you may or may not be right. It's just your own view. However, it does give you the basis of a conversation to check out your accuracy.

Having observed the facts and then started your own perceptive and interpretative process, you may notice that you begin to imagine things about the person. The leader in you might start wondering what their needs are, what might stretch them as a challenge, or what hidden talents they have and how you can unlock their potential.

By observing, perceiving and wondering, you become part of your colleagues' scene, scanning for signals that suggest what to do next. Your role is more like a detective, using your natural curiosity to make sense of what your colleagues need.

Try imagining what it is like to be that person. How might they respond to different situations and what does this imply for your leadership? Best of all, ask them! People will often be glad to tell you what they need, and how they are feeling. By not asking, you ignore an essential source of information that can inform and affect your ability to lead effectively.

Being insightful about others is not just an intuitive gift, it is a skill that can be practised and developed. It will make the difference between whether you struggle to get things done or feel really well supported by a team of colleagues all pulling together to achieve results. Harnessing other people's talents and energy will be a critical focus of your activity.

Social intelligence

Choose a colleague with whom you would like a better working relationship. Now consider your last encounter with them and explore:

- Why did they behave the way they did?
- What were their characteristic actions or speech?
- What were they feeling at the time?
- What did they want?
- What of significance was *not* said during the encounter?
- How did their words differ from their actions?
- What were their actions telling you?
- If you were the person, what would you feel?
- How are you similar to them?
- How are you different from them?
- What motivates that person?
- What would be a challenge for them?
- What would that person really need?

- What would be a great treat for them?
- What is going on in their life outside work?
- How does this affect how they behave?

Seeing what's going on

"We don't see things as they are. We see them as we are."

Anais Nin, author

The third strand underpinning the foundation skill of insight is your ability to see a situation accurately, rather than how you might like it to be. Insight starts with a choice as to where you put your attention. How do you see the big picture of what's going on before making decisions about where to initiate a change?

As with seeing other people, we each view the world through our own mental maze, established over many years. Because of our different experiences no two people ever see the world identically. It's why, for example, some of us see the glass half empty, while others simply see a glass and yet others see one that is half full.

You may have to work quite hard to gain an acute grasp of reality. But once you accurately see what is going on you then have a much better chance of transforming it. When you declare 'This is the situation as I see it' and back it up with factual evidence, people will tend to respond to your picture of the world because it somehow makes sense to them.

In the complex and demanding twenty-first century, there will be a premium for any leader who can adapt and bring insight to often confusing situations. This implies someone who can 'read' the environment, make sense of it and, where necessary, help devise a plan of action.

Faced with uncertainty and disarray, many of us conclude that the world is hopelessly confusing and that it is beyond our ability to affect it significantly. In contrast, as a leader you can be far more positive. Indeed you can be energised by encountering the unknown or the inexplicable. Where others see problems, pitfalls and potential for disaster, you might see opportunity and new possibilities for making a difference.

What stops leaders from seeing the obvious staring them in the face? Eckhard Pfeiffer, Compaq's CEO, failed to listen to the 'B' list of senior managers who urged him time and again to pay attention to upstart PC competitors who were stealing the firm's customers. He preferred his 'A' list of 'yes men' who told him what made him feel comfortable.

The notorious Fred Goodwin refused to listen to warnings that the Royal Bank of Scotland was taking too many risks. Later he thought he could ride out the storm over his pension – 'a reward for failure' – until even he got the message that he had to live in the real world and accept a reduction.

So what will you allow yourself to know? Leadership expert Warren Bennis describes three filters that may distort your picture of reality:[4]

- **The social filter**. You reject information because you do not rate its source. The challenge is: 'How can you be open to information regardless of its source?'

[4] Paul Michelman, 'What leaders allow themselves to know', *Harvard Management Update*, 9 (2), 2004.

- **The contextual filter**. You reject the significance of your surroundings. The challenge is: 'How can you take your environment more fully into account?' For example, are you ignoring or underestimating the power of the organisation's culture?
- **The self-knowledge filter**. Bennis argues that lack of self-knowledge is the most common source of leadership failures. The challenge is: 'How can you learn more about who you are and what causes you to behave as you do?'

In an extreme example of trying to master the filters that obscure reality, Ray Dalio of Bridgewater Associates (the world's largest hedge fund) has a radically transparent approach to investing. He even films internal meetings and allows any employee the chance to openly criticise others – himself included. His company has outperformed all its competitors. His approach is clear: 'Don't believe anything, think for yourself and now let's go through a process of what is true together. But we can't stop that with ego. We can't let that barrier stand in our way.'[5]

These powerful filters seem likely to apply far more in the twenty-first century than in previous periods. They can make you fail to deal with issues you don't want to believe are real, leaving you with skewed vision. What filters might be getting in your way of seeing the world, and how could they be affecting your leadership?

Fighting the filters

Here are some actions you can take to put the filters in their place and ensure you see reality more clearly:

- Stay open to new information by refusing to condemn or reject uncomfortable feedback merely because it comes from a place

[5] Simon Goodley, 'Wacky hedge fund tycoon has the last laugh', *The Guardian*, 10 March 2012.

you do not personally rate highly. For example, if you do not hold certain colleagues in high regard, this does not mean their views or opinions are irrelevant or wrong. Some of the most difficult people may have the most insightful take on what is happening around you.

- Find ways to let others tell you about things that are going on in your own organisation that may affect your choices and leadership decisions. For example, offer people credible ways to give feedback safely, such as via focus groups, surveys or perhaps anonymously. Make it clear you really want to learn about problems that might undermine or delay your plans.
- Get a different perspective on what's going on. For instance, invite people from different departments, disciplines, organisations or industry sectors into your domain to give their views to you. Invite a young person or someone from a different culture in to observe your daily activities and then tell you how they see things. Seeing things through their eyes will help you see the unseen.
- Use mind-mapping as a technique to make sense of the bigger picture. It allows you to use your right brain to visualise what's going on around you and make some connections. For instance, you could put the name of your initiative in the middle of a sheet of paper and start mapping the stakeholders involved. As you do so, you might realise that some of the stakeholders already know each other – which may be a good or a bad thing. It is often these connections that highlight areas that need addressing and possible solutions.

Curiosity

If you are naturally curious, you have the makings of a dynamic leader – one whose insight is powered by a desire to know, to find out more, to learn. This kind of curiosity means you take nothing for granted. Even if it is not broke, you constantly wonder how you can make things better. For instance, you might foster a culture among your team constantly to question results: 'Why did we do better than we expected?' 'Why did we do worse than we expected?' 'How could we do better next time?'

Curiosity can build your insight in various ways:

- Exploring fills you with a sense of adventure – learning how things work and why they work that way. You can't help being excited by the new knowledge!
- Uncertainty does not scare you. Instead it just makes the adventure that much more exciting. You don't judge what you see as good or bad. You simply seek first to understand what it is, what it does, how it works, and why it works that way.
- Unknown to you, your sense of adventure can make it easier for you to learn quickly. And your enthusiasm engages others, causing them to want to explore with you.

"We [scientists] love to be confused because that means we're about to learn something new."

Jeff Forshaw, Professor of Theoretical Physics, University of Manchester

An important aspect to develop is your sensitivity to the behaviour of others. This goes beyond simply understanding them individually. Curiosity about the behaviour of others gives you insight into what works in particular relationships and what doesn't. You do not have to be a psychologist, but you do need to be self-aware and pay close attention to your own actions and to those around you. Otherwise important cues go unexamined and unaddressed, and you risk losing an understanding of critical human aspects that determine the energy and engagement levels in the organisation.

The curious leader

You're a curious leader if you:

- **Ask questions**. These open up the door to new possibilities. Curious leaders don't micromanage with endless questions. Instead, they ask the right ones to move thinking forward.
- **Assume something better is still out there**. A curious mind believes we haven't learned it all, seen it all or done it all. Growth is not only possible, but expected.
- **Are comfortable leading what you don't understand**. A sure way to slow the pace of change and innovation is insisting you must understand every decision, every product and every pixel. Instead, surround yourself with smart people you trust and let them do the work.

Foresight

Leadership also means seeing things as they might be, in the future. If managing is organising what already exists, then leadership is about creating possibilities and moving towards something that does not yet exist.

> "I saw an angel in the stone. And carved to set it free."
>
> **Michelangelo, sculptor, painter and architect**

If you want to know what the future looks like for your organisation, invent it. As a leader you know that while you cannot predict the future you certainly can influence and shape what future your organisation creates for itself. You are therefore looking for relevant shifts in the organisation's environment.

For instance, Carphone Warehouse originally only sold and advised on mobile phones. In response to developing market opportunities and often driven by its leadership insights, it moved on to market broadband, deliver a competitive landline phone service, and has recently launched a music-streaming service and plans to be part of a consortium allowing consumers to see video programmes via the internet.

How can you improve your ability to see new possibilities? Essentially this is about expanding your creative abilities in the widest sense. When leaders use their natural creative powers to see new possibilities, we later look back on what they did and call this form of insight 'foresight'.

To develop your foresight means turning your mind towards the future. For example, in business you need to ask:

- How can we stay ahead of the game?
- What new developments are over the horizon?
- What unexpected situations might we plan for?
- What if current trends were reversed?

Certainly Anita Roddick, the founder of The Body Shop, attributed much of her success to seeing which trends the cosmetics industry was following – and then deliberately going in the opposite direction. Successful financiers who manage investment funds will often say 'we buy when the others are selling; and sell against the trend'.

Looking for alternatives, or examples of counter-cultural activities and where the rules are being broken, often allows you to see what is not yet manifest. Try using these foresight questions with colleagues:

- What are you working on that's new or different?
- If we had a magic wand, how could we transform things around here?

- How could we make things ten times better around here?

Just as it is useful to put yourself in others' shoes and see things from their point of view, so it helps if you can stand outside a situation. Seeing it from afar often allows you to see the bigger picture and not get bogged down in detail. This wider frame of reference often allows you to see where things are going, or how they are developing, rather than being stuck in the current situation.

Insight is seeing, not magic

Certainly some people are born with more insight than others. Yet it is an inherent talent that we all have – it is not magic. You can cultivate it by practising observation, trying to understand other people, attempting to see reality and imagining the future.

For this to happen well, you will need to employ all of your five senses, plus another – which is the sense of wonder. 'Sensory acuity' is the phrase often used to describe your ability to be alert and attentive to what is around us. Another image is summed up by the phrase 'having your antennae working at full strength'. These are all ways of trying to describe the difference between working in a bubble and really being aware of what is going on around you. Insight demands using all your senses to detect and make sense of what is happening.

Spend some time today just looking. Value this space as essential to your leadership and the entire organisation. From periods of reflection come fresh insights that could ensure that people see you as someone who can *lead the way* to future success.

TWITTER SUMMARY

To lead you must see what's needed. Insight is the starting point for action and determines where you focus your energy and initiative.

> **RECAP**
>
> Insight is a mixture of self-awareness, understanding others and really 'seeing' the situation at any moment of time.

IDEAS FOR ACTION

- ✔ Attach more importance to the less logical, more intuitive side of your nature.
- ✔ Set yourself new personal challenges around the whole area of exploring what you are feeling and thinking.
- ✔ Find someone good at knowing what others are thinking and feeling. Spend time talking with them, reviewing recent situations and how they see them. What evidence does this other person use to draw conclusions?
- ✔ Next time you make a decision, talk in a meeting or take an action, try reviewing afterwards: Why did I do that? What effect did I have? Why did that work? How could I do that better? What went wrong with what I did?
- ✔ Identify your internal 'cast of characters'. These aspects of yourself influence how you behave and respond to the world.
- ✔ Widen your perspective. Explore ways of expanding the channels you use for gaining information about the world around you. For example, find opportunities to take a closer look at your views, prejudices, assumptions, beliefs and interpretations.
- ✔ At your next meeting, concentrate on being a careful observer. Use your natural powers of analysis to build a picture of why people do what they do. What are they feeling? What do they want? How do their words differ from their actions? Look closely at their body language – their gestures, posture or expressions.

- ✔ Give yourself a target of attending at least one self-development course every six months. See it as an enjoyable challenge, rather than a burden.
- ✔ Apply your insight to what does not yet exist. Spend more time really thinking about future issues. Insight is partly realising which questions to ask and seeking the answers with the help of others.

03

Initiate

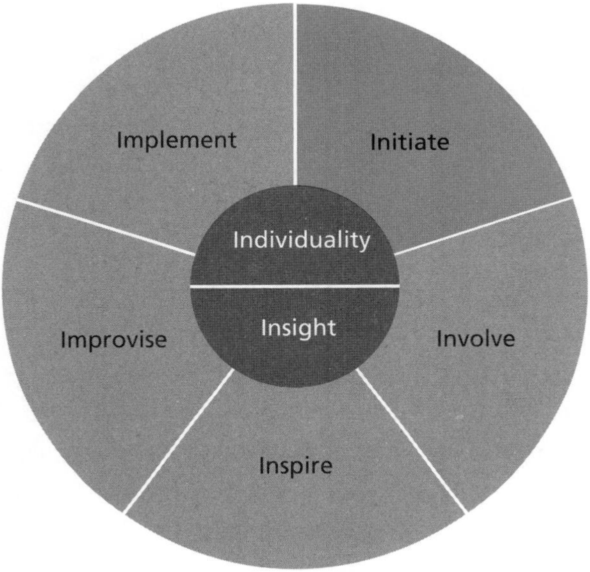

'He was exactly what this company needed, at exactly the right time' explained a lead director on the board of the revived and once-dominant General Motors (GM). Describing his new CEO, this director added: 'He simplified the organisation, reshaped the company's vision, put the right people in place, and brought renewed energy and optimism to GM.'[1]

To *lead the way* you need a strong personal commitment to both setting things in motion and also not waiting for others to give you a sense of direction. This is what we mean by **initiate**. Being 'action-minded' has long been a leadership expectation. But in the rest of this century sustainable leaders like you will need to do more than know the mechanics of setting things in motion.

To initiate change is to be far more proactive – it is an expression of your commitment and passion to improve the situation

[1] GM News, 'GM announces CEO succession process: Dan Akerson to become CEO, Whitacre remains Chairman', 12 August 2010.

around you. It involves a level of self-assurance and sense of direction that ultimately puts your own reputation on the line. At its most basic, it's your ability to turn reflection, information, analysis and management discipline into a sharp instrument of active response. This might have a short- or long-term perspective but the essence is a bias towards making something of value happen.

In the complex world facing companies this century, there will be many pressures to stay risk-averse. Of course there are areas of endeavour where this is appropriate, such as insurance, engineering, health, construction and charitable projects. All of these, and areas such as investment banking, are clearly regulated for a good reason. But there is a danger that many organisations allow their risk-averse systems and processes to prevail in areas where innovation and boldness are requirements.

"Without initiative, leaders are simply workers in leadership positions."

Bo Bennett, author and politician

For some would-be leaders, stepping into the unknown will have few attractions when the world seems so unpredictable. Constant change means never being sure that what you start will result in what you originally intended. How do you feel about this kind of uncertainty? Does it turn your stomach, make you uneasy, or perhaps the reverse? Perhaps it sets your juices flowing. *Leading the way* means you know how to thrive in a world where organisations must be highly flexible, results-oriented and with fast decision-making processes.

Almost everywhere you look organisations seem to be reaching out for leaders who are comfortable with this kind of environment – they are able to handle the anxiety and resistance that may arise. This kind of leadership has the core capability of being able to promote fresh thinking – to initiate. When you initiate something, you do so within a context that might range across a broad landscape, as shown in the box.

The initiative landscape

- **Self**. Questions you might need to explore in this part of the landscape might be: What is your human purpose? Where do you want to go with your life? What do you want your legacy to be? How can you best develop the talents you already possess and find others you never knew you had?

The aim is to seek answers that clarify your purpose, aspirations, intention and desires.

- **People**. No one lives in total isolation. As a leader you will lead people, not just things or an organisation. So part of your initiative will be towards others. It begins with your own honesty about yourself and respect towards other people.

The aim is to create relationships of openness and mutual respect, trust and participation.

- **Ideas**. Another part of the landscape is concerned with ideas. Here you try to bring clarity to what you and others want to achieve. Part of this ability is being able to articulate this vision or these ideas so that others will share your perspective.

The aim is to promote fresh thinking, to advance creativity across the organisation, or at least within your local area of responsibility.

- **Structure**. The structure of your organisation is another important part of the context in which you lead. In this area you may initiate change in terms of how the organisation is structured or arranged.

▶

The aim is to affect the structure so as to influence how the organisation and its components function.

- **Processes**. When you are *leading the way* you need to think about and, if necessary, initiate change in the methods and procedures that underpin purpose and intention.

The aim is to affect the way things get done, not just what gets done.

Taking the initiative can be good for morale, as well raising your own profile within the organisation. Your actions can set you apart from more passive and purely reactive colleagues. When you do initiate change you:

- accept responsibility
- research
- take risks
- instigate direct action
- follow through.

Accept responsibility

"I have always been fallible. I have always felt fallible and I have always acted fallible. If I have a bit of an edge it is because I know what I do not know. I did make a mistake predicting a serious calamity."

George Soros, business magnate, investor and philanthropist

To *lead the way* with initiative means you readily accept responsibility. You can build this capability by constantly seeking new opportunities to volunteer, participate in projects, be accountable for results and take centre stage.

Volunteer

This means saying 'yes' whenever a job needs doing, or a problem needs someone to solve it. Sometimes these will be the worst jobs or the ones with the least apparent kudos. Despite this, step forward and treat these demands as an opportunity, not as 'yet more work'.

For example, be willing to handle a difficult interpersonal issue rife with potential conflict. Or offer to find a solution for some problem that others have failed to resolve or have no time to tackle. When you say 'Yes, I'll do that' you set an example for others and show 'this is how it should be around here.' That is, you demonstrate an aspect of your culture in action. By volunteering, you model how others should perform, and inspire them to take responsibility too. Try saying:

- Leave that to me.
- I'll solve that.
- Nobody else is handling this, so I will.
- I'll be responsible for that.

Participate

Take part in other people's projects. You get a chance to practise your leadership when you willingly join a task force, support a project group, attend a committee, become part of a team activity, and so on. Look for opportunities to add value. This is not always about being in charge. It is more likely to mean collaborating and being part of someone else's leadership initiative.

You can add value in all sorts of ways. You might contribute ideas, take on some of the donkey work, support someone with a task, do some research or simply lend a hand. It's a choice to get involved.

This is proactive participation, where you undertake to do things, rather than merely going along with the crowd, which is a form of passive participation. In contrast, proactive participation shows, by your behaviour, attitude and actions, that you want to contribute.

Be accountable

The famous phrase on the desk of US President Harry S. Truman saying 'The buck stops here!' is a good reminder that as a leader you take responsibility by letting people know you are ultimately accountable. You do this when you tell colleagues:

- I'll make sure that gets done on time.
- That was my fault.
- This won't happen again.
- I give you my word.
- Let's set some specific targets for me.
- This is down to me.

These need to be more than mere words. Tobias Fredberg, a fellow at the TruePoint Center for Higher Ambition Leadership, spent four years studying 36 highly ambitious CEOs from major companies around the world. He concluded that: 'higher-ambition CEOs assume personal responsibility when things are bad and they give collective credit when things are good'.[2]

If you become accountable for a task or project, make sure your levels of responsibility are recorded. Be specific about your commitment and what you are agreeing to. It is then easier, down the line, to measure success and feel proud of your achievements or to be apologetic for any shortfall in results. Don't over-promise and under-deliver.

[2] T. Fredberg, 'Why good leaders pass the credit and take the blame', Harvard Business Review Blog Network, 6 October 2011.

Take centre stage

When you accept the challenge of accountability, you do not blame others, act defensively or hide behind processes. To do so would be disastrous. For example, when Tony Hayward, the ex-CEO of BP, declared in a fit of frustration over the Gulf of Mexico oil spill that 'I want my life back' he failed to accept responsibility, and paid the price by losing the top job.[3]

As Hayward discovered the hard way, you cannot be a leader and remain a shrinking violet. Ultimately, you must be willing to stand in the limelight of people's attention. To be an effective leader means being prepared to be visible – in whatever form that takes.

For some leaders this turns into a narcissistic approach to being in charge. However, it need not be that way. Progressive leaders are visible, but not because they are self-serving or attention seeking. They just want to demonstrate accountability. As the seminal study on outstanding companies by Jim Collins found, high-level leaders are a portrait of duality: modest yet wilful, humble yet fearless.[4]

Research

Before you embark on any initiative take time to identify the stakeholders who will be involved in the process. They are the context for the action you are about to instigate. Finding out in advance how they might respond to the initiative is an important part of your planning process. So open the communication channels with your stakeholders as soon as possible.

[3] *The Times*, 'Embattled BP chief: I want my life back', 31 May 2010.

[4] Jim Collins, *Good to Great*, Random House, 2001.

Few attempts at communication within an organisation succeed if they simply inform people without really hearing what they think and feel about what is being attempted. An often neglected aspect of initiating is therefore the ability to really listen hard to what others say.

Effective listening

Listen so you can:

- pick up on problems before they get out of hand
- uncover the causes of miscommunication and conflict
- understand people's motives, values and feelings
- build rapport and mutual respect
- discover trends that drive how business gets done
- gather and evaluate ideas
- generate solutions.

Focusing on your stakeholders will give you information that will make your chances of a successful initiative infinitely better. It is always worth taking some time to explore the impact of your initiative on the people who will be involved in it. Ask yourself:

- How will they be affected by the initiative?
- What questions will they ask?
- What are the barriers and challenges they will face?
- What's in it for them? (What are the benefits?)
- What's *not* in it for them? (What are the problems and losses?)
- How well do you know them?
- Who might support you in influencing them?

"If you want to persuade me you've got to think my thoughts, feel my feelings and speak my words."

Cicero, Roman orator

Take risks

In 2009 the consulting firm Booz & Company helped GM department chiefs to identify middle managers who were unafraid to take risks. You might think that these would be confident, high-powered executives or those on the 'fast track'. In fact they were often maverick types, who knew how to get things done by manipulating the system so as to get things done right.[5]

While leaders commonly endorse the virtues of risk-taking, in practice many cannot tolerate mistakes and tend to punish daring. There is often a wide gap between rhetoric and reality. This inability to take risks usually arises from fear of failure, losing control and attracting criticism. However, there will far less room for this type of behaviour in successful companies in the rest of this century. If you work in an organisation that punishes risk-taking or clings to the status quo then, as a leader, you will 'need a dose of extra courage' as one report on innovation observed.[6] Future successful organisations will need not only courageous leaders, but ones who are comfortable with risk.

There is also an important distinction between being risky and being reckless. Those who *lead the way* will appreciate the difference – for them risk-taking is part of the creative aspect of their role. For example, the CEO of the Royal Bank of Scotland, Fred Goodwin, was reckless, because his leadership eventually

[5] John Baldoni, 'How to buck the system the right way', *Fast Company*, 16 March 2010.

[6] Blessing White Intelligence, *Innovate on the Run: The Competing Demands of Modern Leadership*, 2007.

undermined the entire existence of the organisation. Contrast that with the risk run by Tesco's Terry Leahy in choosing to enter the US market where so many others have failed. The venture, still unproven, was merely a reasonable business gamble, not a matter of corporate survival.

Adversity is often a great stimulus to responsible risk-taking. Faced with a supplier who was demanding excessive prices, the entrepreneur James Dyson refused to be held to ransom and to the supplier's amazement made alternative arrangements. This was certainly risky but not reckless. Similarly, Eric Schmidt, who famously turned round the fortunes of Novell, was unafraid to run risks to alter the company's performance. 'You know it's a natural reaction to turn cautious when your company's in trouble', he said, 'but that's precisely the wrong tack to take. You have to give your people freedom to pursue their passions. That's the only way to keep them focused and inspired.'[7]

Step out of your comfort zone

As we have said, people learn through experience. New experiences, especially, tend to feel uncomfortable. However, if you have ever had a very powerful or challenging experience in your life, you are likely to look back on it with the realisation that it changed you in some way. You were never quite the same again. It is one of life's potent lessons.

Stepping into leadership is often one of those powerful new experiences and is likely push you out of your comfort zone. So, you might as well prepare yourself as best as you can so that you stand a good chance of not just surviving, but thriving. This can be an exhilarating process, as you set out to make something important happen.

Future successful organisations will have a great need for leaders who are willing to take on potentially scary assignments. High

[7] Daniel Goleman, 'What makes a leader?', *Harvard Business Review*, January 2004.

levels of uncertainty demand a different kind of leader than during times of stability and minimal change. We can expect these organisations to seek leaders willing to experiment, put themselves in danger of failing, be ready to do what others least expect, and to do what is right.

If stepping out of your comfort zone fills you with dread, it is time to start practising. That is how you will start developing the internal psychological resources to deal with it. The more often you do take on new experiences, the less uncomfortable it will feel. It will probably never feel easy, but at least it won't stop you. Practising can take many forms. For example, here are some challenges that other leaders have found useful:

- **Physical challenges**: ride in a hot air balloon, be a blood donor, make a bungee jump, go dancing somewhere strange.
- **Social challenges**: attend an unusual sporting event, help disabled kids, organise a community activity.
- **Emotional challenges**: confront somebody with a difficult truth, express honest feelings to a person.
- **Political challenges**: phone a talk radio show, make a speech, support a local charity campaign.

Can you think of some activities that might make you feel stretched and challenged?

Twenty ways to step out of your comfort zone

1 Disagree with someone important.

2 Raise money for a charity.

3 Tell someone you care about that you care about them.

4 Break the rules.

5 Challenge convention.

▶

6 Try new things.

7 Do what's right, not what's expected.

8 Spend a day navigating around your organisation in a wheelchair.

9 Act without always knowing the likely outcomes.

10 Deliberately put yourself in a learning situation.

11 Ask five people for feedback about your leadership style.

12 Commit to action without knowing if others will support you.

13 Choose 12 challenging experiences and complete one for each month of the year.

14 Disrupt old patterns and habits – take a different route home for once, read a paper you hate, drink a different brand of beer, get up each day at a different time.

15 Spend a day with the least well-paid person in your organisation.

16 Give up chairing your team meeting for six months.

17 Ask for a list of anyone who has complained about your product or service and personally ring and apologise – really listen to why they are annoyed.

18 Share your favourite poem with everyone and explain why it is special to you.

19 Invite a school leaver to attend your team meeting and critique it.

20 Invite suggestions from around the organisation on expanding this list.

If a voice inside keeps saying 'This is a waste of time', that is why you would benefit from being given a shake-up, and some help to see the world afresh.

Be assertive

Sometimes speaking up in a meeting and asserting your point of view feels very risky. In fact, every time you *lead the way*, you are asserting yourself and what you believe to be the right thing to do. In doing so you will always risk lack of agreement or even disapproval. Nevertheless, if you have something to offer that will add value, then you need to assert yourself.

Many leaders, however, consider themselves assertive when in reality they are aggressive or secretly defensive. For example, outspoken Michael O'Leary, head of Ryanair, takes no prisoners and always seems confident. Yet something in his manner might suggest that perhaps he is rather less certain of himself than he would have us believe. And what can we conclude from the response by ex-Channel Five chief executive Dawn Airey on being asked why she was the CEO: 'I'm just bloody good!'?

The need to promote collaboration, virtual teams, flatter organisations and talented employees suggests there will be declining tolerance in future successful organisations for seriously aggressive or nasty leaders. Instead, there will be a growing demand for assertive leaders able to resist pressure to do what is expected, but willing to say what they think is right, and initiate it without appearing aggressive or intolerant of others' views.

Research suggests that being seen as under- or over-assertive may be the most common weakness among aspiring leaders.[8]

Handle reverses

"Ever tried. Ever failed. No matter. Try again. Fail again. Fail better."

Samuel Beckett, playwright

[8] *Science Daily*, 'What makes a good leader: the assertiveness quotient', 5 February 2007.

Dealing with rejection, disagreement and failure is another way leaders show initiative. How do *you* handle these inevitable experiences? What happened last time when things failed to go your way? Did your reactions undermine your leadership confidence? How readily did you bounce back after facing adversity?

In the face of rejection or failure, effective leaders use various ways to sustain their morale. For example, they use techniques such as persistence and keeping many projects going simultaneously. Few of us succeed in life without some setbacks or finding that some people disagree with us. There remains a fundamental truth in the famous IBM adage: 'To double your successes, double your failures'.

Non-personalising is another effective way leaders persist with their initiatives. That is, they realise that setbacks are seldom aimed at them personally. Instead, they acknowledge that most arise from forces beyond their immediate control.

Reframing is yet another useful method. For example, suppose you conclude that your organisation is weak on marketing and needs to invest in a new approach. If your idea hits resistance, rather than give up, you might reframe the issue as 'a need to conduct an experiment to learn more about what works in marketing terms'. Repositioning the issue in this way and re-presenting the cost as the price of learning may change other people's reactions.

Instigate direct action

How focused are you on action? For example, people differ in their leadership preferences. Some like to push for short-term, tangible action; others enjoy communicating and making contact with people; others are most comfortable with planning, long-term strategy and innovation; and yet others lean towards administration, with their attention on systems, procedures and details.

Action-minded leadership

If your style is action-minded, you

- make things happen rather than just talk about them
- motivate and engage
- communicate your intentions openly and widely
- persistently follow through
- constantly seek feedback on what is happening
- seek out information about divergence from expected norms
- rely on relationships to underpin action
- insist on seeing for yourself that the right things are happening.

How much of this do you do? What is the balance you strike between being action-minded and allowing time for reflection about an issue before initiating action? Do people regard you as action-minded?

When it comes to direct action, the commercial world can learn a lot from campaigning activists in the voluntary sector. Take Franny Armstrong and Lizzie Gillett for instance. Having made the powerful climate-change documentary called *The Age of Stupid*, uniquely financed by 'crowd funding', they then came up with the idea of challenging people and organisations to cut their carbon emissions by 10 per cent in one year. The idea took hold and soon thousands of individuals, companies, organisations, towns and even countries joined the 10:10 campaign and signed up to the commitment.

And then there's Eugenie Harvey who created 'We Are What We Do', a brand and movement that she launched in 2004 with the book *Change the World for a Fiver*. A serial initiator, she then started the 'I'm Not a Plastic Bag' project, which has led to an increase in awareness about unnecessary plastic bag usage all over the world. The movement recently published *Change the World at 35,000 ft* in collaboration with Virgin Atlantic, and in 2010 they brought out *31 Ways to Change the World* – a book created by children and young people.

Sometimes it is important to simply get an initiative under way so that it can leverage support and grow in its impact. For instance, a small group of people at the philanthropic charity Network for Social Change was concerned about the crippling levels of third-world debt. They raised money for a researcher to explore what could be done. This then led to a lobbying campaign to influence key decision makers. Within a few years their plans were adopted by the global Jubilee 2000 campaign and resulted in the removal of billions of pounds of African debt.

> "Whatever you can do or dream you can, begin it. For boldness has genius, power and magic in it. Begin it now!'
>
> **Johann Wolfgang von Goethe, writer and polymath**

Follow through

How good are you at following through? This is the Achilles heel of many leaders and can potentially be the source of a myriad of problems: botched projects, broken trust with employees and higher-ups, wasted money and time, and even lay-offs or firings. Become an expert at following through, either doing it yourself or making sure others do it on your behalf.

Secrets of successful follow-through

- Keep meticulous task lists.
- Hold regular meetings to monitor and progress-chase.
- Organise thoughts and activities clearly.
- Take time out to reflect.
- Do not operate in crisis mode.
- Know who needs to be in the loop.
- Know who is accountable for what.
- Have a fundamental desire to complete things.

It is common to find weak follow-through on new initiatives. Each initiative is piled on top of another with seldom a systematic review of whether it is succeeding, failing or has adequate support. The result is scepticism about each new initiative. A common reaction of people is consequently: 'Don't respond to this new one – there'll be another along in a minute!'

For instance, when a new chairman of Shell was appointed some years ago, he reviewed the initiatives of all those in whose footsteps he was following. Without exception, he discovered they too had conducted reviews, followed by announcements of major new programmes of change. Yet his research showed that virtually none of the previous initiatives had taken hold. He was confronting the raw truth that in senior positions one easily becomes a prisoner – marooned in the executive suite – handling the tidal flood of information, requests and communication, rather than initiating and pursuing anything of substance.

In contrast, when BP's new CEO took over in 2010 he promised, like his luckless predecessor, to change the company's safety culture. But he did more than proclaim the intention. He geared fourth-quarter employee bonuses to whether people were turning the intention into a reality.

Taking the initiative is not enough. You need to back it up with tangible follow-through.

TWITTER SUMMARY

Having identified what needs to be done, you initiate changes. This can be risky and exhilarating.

RECAP

Most successful leaders show initiative and value it in other people by recognising environment shifts, accepting responsibility, researching the situation, taking risks, instigating direct action and following through.

IDEAS FOR ACTION

- ✔ Put yourself forward on a regular basis – volunteering for those jobs others reject.
- ✔ Tackle the jobs you keep putting off because you're too busy, or because they seem too difficult.
- ✔ Participate more in other people's projects, for example by being more ready to join a task force, a project team or a committee. Be sure your involvement is active not passive.
- ✔ Give more attention to being accountable – demonstrating that you can really be relied upon.
- ✔ Start letting people hear from you such phrases as: 'I'll see that gets done'; 'Leave that to me'; 'I got that wrong'; 'I'll complete that on time'; 'I take responsibility for that'.

- ✔ Research the likely impact of any initiative on your stakeholders.
- ✔ Seek more opportunities to step out of your comfort zone; be assertive; and handle rejection, disagreement and failure.
- ✔ List 12 challenging things you would like to do yet have never done before. Complete one of these each month, for a year.
- ✔ To help maintain your morale when facing setbacks, use techniques such as persistence, non-personalising, reframing, and keeping many balls in the air.
- ✔ Follow through on initiatives.

04

Involve

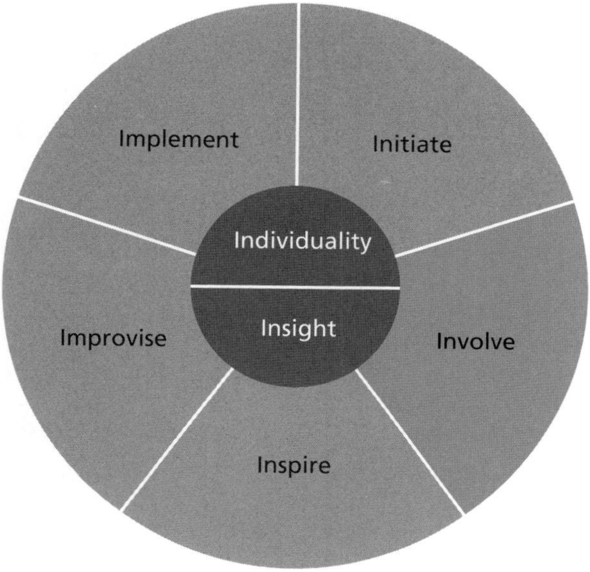

In Elizabethan times you might never have noticed someone slipping a coin into your beer. When you found it at the bottom of the glass it was too late. You had inadvertently accepted the 'Queen's shilling' and consequently been legally enrolled in Her Majesty's Navy. But it is not easy to force someone to be involved so that they readily accept what others want them to do. Most press-ganged victims made poor sailors and deserted as soon as they could.

Press gangs merely highlight the real difference between involvement and full-hearted engagement and commitment when people choose to give of their best. As Martina Navratilova, the tennis star, once put it, to understand the difference between involvement and commitment, 'Just think of bacon and eggs'. She said: 'The hen is involved but the pig is committed!'

Leaders who know how to involve people seldom do it out of pure kindness, but because it has a practical result. It can be highly transformative. Their 'democratic' form of leadership creates satisfaction, awareness, new ways of thinking, and outstanding performance. This ideally suits the emerging needs of twenty-first-century organisations. We can therefore expect a growing demand for this particular leadership capability, in contrast to the old style of leadership.

Old and new leadership

Old-style leadership	Shared or involving leadership
You're a leader because of your position in a group or hierarchy.	You're a leader because of your ability to create quality interactions between people.
You're judged as a leader by whether you solve problems.	You're judged as a leader by how people are working together.
You are responsible for providing solutions and answers.	Everyone plays a part in getting results; you enable this process.
There is a distinct difference between you the leader and your 'followers', through character and skills.	People are interdependent, all actively contributing to the process of leadership.
Communication tends to be formal, rather than conversational.	Communication is central, with a stress on conversation and dialogue.
You may see secrecy, deception, coercion and pay-offs as acceptable ways of making things happen.	You are driven by values in which honesty and shared ethics are paramount and you seek the common good.

"Leadership is about constantly thinking: 'What can I do for the team to help them achieve what I want them to achieve?'"

Tracy Edwards, skipper of the first round-the-world all-female crew

As a leader, your attraction to organisations will mainly depend on whether you can involve people. Why? Because this ability provides you with the resources needed to transform situations. At its most basic, people voluntarily participate in what you want to achieve. At its most advanced, anyone can contribute to the leadership role through their willingness to be accountable for results, using their unique knowledge, skills, character, connections and determination. The diagram illustrates this involvement spectrum.

Level 1: Participation and enrolment

- I'll take part
- I agree to contribute
- Yes, I'll give it attention
- I'll be there
- I feel I know what's going on around here
- I can generally influence decisions where it affects my work

↓

Level 2: Engagement

- I'm really enthusiastic about it
- It has my full attention
- I absolutely believe in this
- We really need to know a lot more about this
- I'll do my level best
- If I have an idea they will listen and take notice

↓

Level 3: Commitment

- There's no turning back now
- Let's do whatever it takes to make it happen
- We'll go the extra mile
- I'll surpass myself if I can
- Why don't we stay late and fix it?

↓

Level 4: Leadership

- I'll make it happen
- I'll be accountable for that
- This is down to me now
- This is what I want to achieve
- Here's what I want us to do

Intensity of involvement

The ways in which you involve or engage people in what you want to achieve are essentially simple. First, you need to recognise the value of involving people. Second, you must choose practical ways to go about achieving it. Third, you need to initiate action that creates it.

Participation and enrolment

Creating basic participation is usually the easiest part of the involvement journey. At this low level of intensity, people may at least offer token compliance. That is, they are willing to go through the motions of involvement. For example, they may say they support what you want to do, attend your meetings, nominally accept work assignments, and so on. But it is only with actual engagement, commitment and beyond that you can expect to see transformative performance by both individuals and the organisation.

When someone enrols in your vision or intention, they become sufficiently committed to offer support. This usually occurs once people start to understand what you want to achieve, and realise they can be part of the grand design, with a possible role.

Enrolling support

- Communicate purpose: 'This is what I need you to do and why it matters ...'
- Ask them to join you in working towards the goal: 'Will you try to achieve this ...?'
- Explain clearly why you need their help: 'This will only be possible if you ...'
- Describe how they can personally affect the outcome: 'If you do this, it will result in ...'

- Invite them to say what they need to in order to feel enrolled: 'What will it take to get your full support?'
- Describe how the end result will affect them personally: 'What's in it for you?'
- Say what will be the likely consequences of not enrolling: 'Without your active help, it could mean that you ...'

Only when people fully grasp what you want to achieve can they make up their minds to 'buy in'. This is partly why all effective leaders choose to become powerful communicators. They know how important it is to learn the art of persuasion and how to make a verbal impact. Is this your strong or weak area? If necessary, consider investing in some presentation coaching.

Apart from putting the message across well, you can encourage enrolment through directly asking people if they will join with you in your scheme. This is not seeking their permission, rather it is checking whether they wish to participate in the grand design. Invite people to tell you what they require to feel enrolled. It might be anything from a hefty salary to a challenging job, from time off to care for a dependent to the opportunity to job share. Never take people's enrolment for granted, even if you originally employed them. Try to uncover what they themselves feel would make them committed to the purpose.

Two of the most powerful ways leaders obtain people's enrolment are by showing people they will be engaged in something extraordinary, and clarifying the value of their personal contribution.

You cannot expect people to enrol if what's on offer is dull or pedestrian. It must capture their imagination and make them feel the risks along the way will somehow be worth it. Develop the knack of explaining how even the simplest tasks link to the grand design. One reason James Dyson insists that everyone joining his company spends a day learning to assemble his breakthrough vacuum cleaner is that it helps them relate directly and viscerally to the manufacturing and design purpose that is driving the company.

By showing people how their contribution will make a difference to whatever you are wanting to achieve, you bring alive for each person the part they can play, no matter how small or indirect. An example of this happens in Disney theme parks. In Disneyland the employees most often approached by visitors for help and directions are those tasked with keeping the place clean. They are no longer lowly sweepers, but important contributors of information and advice. Similarly, in an international logistics company the leaders realised that employees most often interacting with its customer base were not its office staff but its delivery drivers. Previously treated almost as cannon fodder, 'Just doing my job, mate', they were promoted to customer liaison staff, given additional training and ongoing support.

The importance of clarifying why you need someone's help is underlined by David Barrass, an experienced interim chief executive specialising in turnaround roles at struggling businesses. He has described how, when working at the Royal Mint, 'The first couple of managerial meetings I held, it was just me saying, "this is what I want, here are the targets I am setting for us and that I am committing to the Treasury that we will deliver."' Yet 'within six months he had brought people with him and the pronoun changed from "I" to "we".'[1]

It helps if you say why you need help. Don't assume employees realise their job is to contribute. If you want more than passive compliance, in which people apparently go along with what you want, be willing to explain fully how their support can make all the difference.

[1] C. Chynoweth, 'Real chiefs get their hands dirty', *Sunday Times*, 3 October 2010.

Why engage?

Engagement goes beyond mere enrolment or participation. With engagement people will go that extra mile and the benefits flow to both them and the organisation. For example, Gallup sifted through data from around 200,000 employees in 36 organisations and across 21 industries. It found levels of employee engagement directly affected five key business outcomes: productivity, profitability, customer loyalty, employee retention and safety. There are plenty of other studies showing a clear relationship between employee engagement and key company financial metrics.[2]

Similarly, UK research in the NHS showed staff engagement as a critical factor for delivering a successful service. For example, shared influence over decision making in teams resulted in lower levels of patient mortality, while staff involvement and improved job satisfaction led to improved team and patient satisfaction.[3]

There is often a long way to go before many organisations fully engage their staff and utilise the potential for better performance. A UK study by the consultancy company Towers Perrin showed that only 12 per cent of UK employees were highly engaged, 65 per cent moderately engaged and 23 per cent disengaged. Moving people up the engagement scale can therefore have a large effect on performance.[4] Similar low levels of engagement have been found in more wide-ranging global studies.

[2] See, for example, David MacLeod and Nita Clarke, *Engaging for Success: Enhancing Performance Through Employee Engagement*, Department of Business, Innovation and Skills, 2009.

[3] Department of Health, *Staff Involvement: Better Decisions, Better Care*, 2003.

[4] Navisys, *The Case for Increasing Employee Engagement*, Navisys Transformation, 2007.

How to engage people

How do you move your people beyond compliance or participation towards engagement? There are some basic steps to take for winning commitment and engagement. One useful approach is called VIDI[5] – shorthand for saying that people need to feel:

- Valued
- Involved
- Developed
- Inspired.

This is both a checklist and a plan of action. These four core requirements offer a route map for winning engagement.[6]

Being valued

One of the deepest hungers of the human heart is to be seen and understood – in simple terms, to be feel valued. This has great resonance in the twenty-first century when so many people feel alienated and disassociated from the world around them. To value those around you and gain their engagement, start seeing them as individuals and reflect this in your leadership actions. This is a particular challenge for anyone leading a large organisation, yet talented leaders still manage to create a culture where individuals feel valued for what they bring to the party.

Many leaders think the only way of valuing people is to pay them more. If these leaders' budget is tight, they feel stymied and impotent. And yet so much research shows that money is rarely the sole motivator for people's commitment. As has been said, 'In

[5] From the Latin *videre* (to see): leaders need to see what people need in order to engage them.

[6] See, for example, Maynard Leigh Associates, *Talent Engagement: How to Unlock People's Potential*, 2010.

difficult times when you have to be financially stingy, you can at least be emotionally generous'. Acknowledgment, recognition and appreciation really don't cost that much.

In our own company we used to have a box of gifts called 'the above and beyond box'. At any time, when a team member felt a colleague had contributed something beyond their role, they could call the team to order and announce the presentation of an award. The recipient would then select a present from the box. It was a small gesture, but helped people to feel recognised and appreciated.

People want to feel valued for who they are – their individuality. This means you need to encourage an environment where your people feel they have a unique contribution to make. It is where, as a leader, you:

- encourage and recruit diversity
- treat others with respect
- avoid using stereotypes
- make it clear that prejudice is wrong
- don't allow bigoted comments by others to go unchallenged.

Paying attention to how employees live their working lives and helping them to improve is a sound investment if you want to involve them in your goals. Valuing their unique individuality also requires paying attention to their well-being and work–life balance. In an era of 24/7 communication some might argue this is no longer possible – that rather than a work–life balance we can now only expect a perpetual digital hum governing our existence. But such a view abandons any responsibility for people's well-being or the need to establish a humane environment in which people can flourish.

One of the biggest obstacles to people feeling valued is the lack of trust. Studies around the world show extremely low levels of trust between leaders and their colleagues. You can build trust by keeping your promises and behaving with integrity, but also by trusting and empowering your people. If you believe in them, then they are likely to feel valued.

Being involved

Winning people's involvement is another important step along the way to gaining their engagement. It is now high on the agenda of many far-sighted organisations and will almost certainly continue to be so for many years. For example, in the UK the O_2 organisation employs a 'head of employee involvement', while the retailer Marks & Spencer has a permanent Business Involvement Group (BIG). It ensures people have an opportunity to voice their views and ideas. Similarly, the John Lewis partnership, long one of the UK's most successful retail concerns, has always recognised involvement as its secret formula for survival and growth.

The amazing turnaround at ITV started when CEO Adam Crozier and his HR team launched an initiative called 'Let's Get Engaged'. He kicked it off with a series of road-shows. Staff were invited to contribute ideas for improvements. The leadership received 9,000 notes with suggestions. Employees certainly felt involved at the prospect of being able to make a difference. The HR team followed up with responses to every single idea and each month communicated news of action that had resulted from the suggestions.

Communication plays a key role in creating involvement, but only around a third of employees feel their leaders communicate openly and honestly. Rigid communication channels and a culture of keeping information hidden all contribute to switching off people's involvement.

Try to keep the communication as open as possible. At Happy Ltd, an award-winning computer training company, all finances are open for everyone to see, including everyone's salaries. Open communication keeps people involved and facilitates better relationships. Find out what people really want to know and, unless there is a very good reason for secrecy, make the information available.

Being developed

As children we can hardly help but develop. Growing and developing is a natural human drive and should continue throughout life. The smart organisations realise that and encourage it. Even so, development is often seen as a 'nice to have' rather than an essential. While some organisations may provide simple skills training, they miss out on investing in someone's long-term growth.

In contrast, if you give careful attention to your people's development needs, not just their training requirements, you demonstrate a commitment to them. And the same goes for career advancement. Make sure that everyone has a personal development plan evolved from discussions with them and review work allocation to ensure people are fully stretched and challenged.

Being inspired

We tend to assume leaders are meant to inspire us. Yet few do. In our development work in companies, both nationally and globally, many leaders we encounter have either forgotten how, or lost the drive to excite and uplift their people. For instance, only 10 per cent of American business professionals are inspired and few look forward to going to work – and most point to a lack of leadership as the problem.[7] But inspiration is an important driver of engagement – we look at it in more detail in the next chapter.

Meetings

In theory, meetings can help you win people's involvement. In practice, most meetings are notoriously dull and boring. One recent study even found attending them makes you stupid by

[7] See, for example, Carmine Gallo, 'The seven secrets of inspiring leaders', *Bloomberg Businessweek*, 10 October 2007.

lowering your intelligence![8] When you add in the complications of conference calls, video-conferencing and other technologically driven variations, the problems mount up. Yet it doesn't have to be that way. Live meetings are a rare opportunity for a group of people to get together and produce 'more than the sum of the parts'. If managed well, a meeting can be an exciting creative process where there is indeed a meeting of minds and even hearts.

You can use meetings to get everyone present involved, by distributing responsibility, encouraging debate, sharing ideas and building relationships. Even conference-call meetings, with clever planning, can include creative elements such as problem solving, brainstorming, sharing examples of inspirational performance and personal disclosure.

Meetings are expensive because normally the time of everyone present is being paid for. So, they are worth investing in. You can bring humanity and creativity to your meetings by making sure they really do provide a space where people can connect, contribute, feel they belong and become involved.

Running dynamic meetings

- **Clarify the purpose of the meeting.** Don't run a meeting unless it has an important purpose, for example to make decisions, build relationships, plan for the future, gain commitment for action, etc. If it's just about operational information exchange then that can be done by email.

[8] See, for example, Uncommondescent.com, 'Human intelligence diminishes in group tasks', January 2012 (commenting on a study at the Virginia Tech Carilion Research Institute).

- **Invite vital attendees**. Many meetings fail or are boring because they are not relevant for many of the people who attend. Make sure everyone who is there is attending because their presence makes a difference.
- **Send information in advance**. Prepare for the meeting by distributing the agenda and background information beforehand. Reach an agreement that no item can be on the agenda without background information. And that people cannot contribute to the agenda item unless they have read the information in advance.
- **Use agendas**. The agenda should state the desired outcome of each point. Is the point for information, discussion, decision or action? Provide an estimate of the time allowed for each item.
- **Encourage participation**. Ask different people to speak on different items on the agenda. Perhaps ask people to prepare papers in advance.
- **Rotate the chair**. Get different people to chair different meetings. And ask each person to bring something new to the process.
- **Keep a focus of attention**. Make sure people are fully present and attentive during the meeting, not distracted, doodling or on mobile devices.
- **Be creative**. Meetings are great opportunities for creative collaboration. Put a strict time limit on creative activity so that it does not go on too long. Try running the meeting in a different environment.
- **Use energy**. Keep the meeting dynamic by ensuring participation and varying the energy.
- **Clarify action points**. Make sure there is no ambiguity about what has been agreed or decided.

Empowerment

"When the best leader's work is done, the people say: 'We did it ourselves'".

Lao Tzu, philosopher of ancient China

Ordering someone to 'be involved' is like shouting at a plant to 'grow'! The ultimate aim of involvement is to allow people to move from a culture of control to one where they can take responsibility. Having the autonomy to take over all aspects of managing their work, including holiday scheduling, ordering materials and hiring new team members, can produce spectacular gains in productivity and creativity.

The days of command and control leadership are rapidly ending. Leadership in the twenty-first century is more about sharing your power and giving support to your people so they feel inspired to do great things. You see empowerment at work in self-managed teams where people are allowed to take more charge of their lives and their work. There the leadership moves around, and everyone feels permitted to take on aspects of the leader's role. It is a bit like a theatre ensemble or a chamber orchestra. No one is totally in charge. Instead, everyone works collaboratively and takes collective responsibility for leadership.

Paradoxically, by handing over some of your leadership authority you do not diminish it, you actually enhance it. People then feel more able to ask for your help, to hear your suggestions and to follow your lead. Some of the known results arising from empowering others include:

- energising jaded employees
- increasing morale

- raising productivity
- improving quality
- reduced staff turnover.

There are countless ways you might empower others through your leadership. Some well-tried ones include:

- Show people they're part of the management and can help the organisation improve.
- Ensure ideas are appreciated, even if they are not always implemented.
- Trust people with responsibility.
- Respect people's ideas and judgement.
- Allow people to make decisions around their own area of work responsibility.
- Give them a budget to manage – with generous sign-off levels.

Tools for empowerment

- Team talks – listening to those on the coalface.
- Listening lunches – a monthly lunch for the leader and staff at all levels.
- Management by walking about: just asking questions and listening.
- Fortnightly department meetings.
- Monthly one-to-one meetings with line managers.
- Quarterly have-your-say questionnaire.
- Three-monthly employee meetings bringing people together from different locations.
- Newsletters and video casts every month, plus regular feedback.

- Open chatroom via email.
- Moderated chatroom on the website, where anyone can post a question.
- Daily news release on the intranet to keep people informed of what's going on.

Both enrolment and involvement are easier to achieve if people have a personal investment in the vision or purpose. When someone has something at stake and a personal commitment they are less likely to fall by the wayside and cease to support your project. This personal investment is rarely financial, but rather about putting important aspects of themselves into the work. This might include their:

- time
- energy
- creativity
- ideas
- know-how
- reputation
- promotion prospects
- personal resources such as information and contacts
- personal development
- formal training.

When you demonstrate you also have a major personal investment in the vision or purpose, others are more likely to join in.

Coaching

Coaching can be a highly effective way of promoting involvement. It brings you in close proximity with a person – normally on a one-to-one basis. The focus is usually on developing people, helping them achieve outstanding results and through that becoming more involved.

How coaching helps create involvement

- **Retention**. Coaching helps retain talent; people increasingly expect leaders to be willing to coach.
- **Personal needs**. People are able to find solutions and meaningful goals for themselves.
- **Immediacy**. You can tackle issues as they arise and manage performance.
- **Recognition**. Through personal attention, people come to feel valued and 'seen'.
- **Advancement**. People can see their place in any succession planning.

Coaching is well established in around 90 per cent of companies, according to the CIPD in the UK. Learning to coach is likely to be in high demand in twenty-first-century organisations that attach importance to getting the best from their people. True, coaching is time-consuming and requires a personal commitment to master the basics. But by using it you build people's confidence to become more engaged, committed and ready to take new levels of responsibility, such as being willing to coach others.

How ready are you to coach? Do you feel fully equipped to do this type of work with colleagues? Coaching is not just a technique, it's a relationship. You don't 'do' coaching to someone; it's a two-way affair in which both of you learn. You can learn dozens of 'how to's' for coaching, but the most important one is your willingness to make it into a mutual development experience.

Why bother with coaching when in the short term it is simpler and quicker just to tell someone what to do? If you can guide, prompt and stimulate the other person to decide for themselves what to do, they won't be constantly coming back to you. Quite simply, coaching is a good investment of your time.

A coaching session can broadly cover five stages, as shown in the diagram.

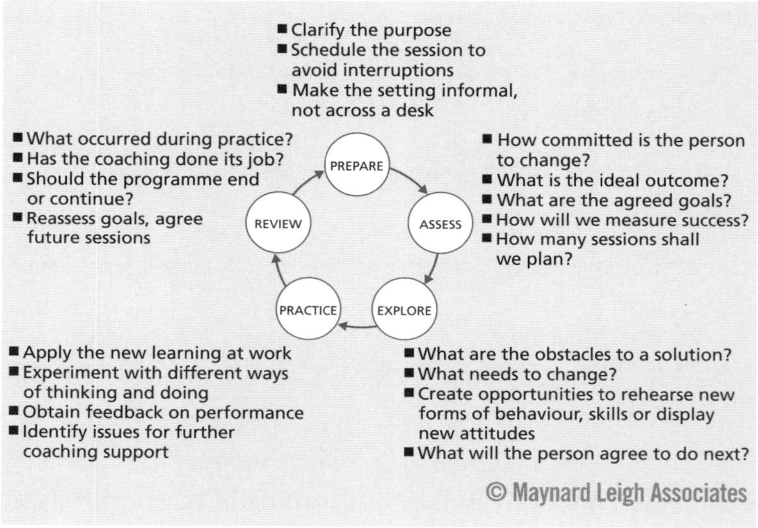

■ Clarify the purpose
■ Schedule the session to avoid interruptions
■ Make the setting informal, not across a desk
PREPARE
ASSESS
■ How committed is the person to change?
■ What is the ideal outcome?
■ What are the agreed goals?
■ How will we measure success?
■ How many sessions shall we plan?
EXPLORE
■ What are the obstacles to a solution?
■ What needs to change?
■ Create opportunities to rehearse new forms of behaviour, skills or display new attitudes
■ What will the person agree to do next?
PRACTICE
■ Apply the new learning at work
■ Experiment with different ways of thinking and doing
■ Obtain feedback on performance
■ Identify issues for further coaching support
REVIEW
■ What occurred during practice?
■ Has the coaching done its job?
■ Should the programme end or continue?
■ Reassess goals, agree future sessions
© Maynard Leigh Associates

Five stages in a coaching session

Each of the stages requires you to do certain actions. For example, in assessing someone's willingness to change you need to discover how committed they are to this. Or when it comes to practising you will need to identify further issues where coaching support might be useful.

Coaching is an area where you can usefully get help both to learn and to practise your technique.

One of the best ways of using coaching is in informal situations where there is not enough time to prepare for an in-depth session. Informal coaching can take place at any time, anywhere.

Somebody might meet you in the coffee area and ask to have ten minutes of your time as they need a bit of coaching.

In these circumstances, you can use action-focused coaching and can obtain value from even a five- or ten-minute encounter. This approach has an attractive logic and simplicity. You work through three stages with the other person:

- objective
- obstacles
- action.

In each case you encourage the other person to explore the implications, and you help them with carefully directed questions to prompt their thinking in new directions.

Giving people a voice

One way managers and leaders have traditionally encouraged involvement is through offering an 'ever-open door'. Supposedly, any supporter can walk through this and raise issues or share concerns. Yet the reality is rather different. Probably less than one in five employees feel they experience an open door and instead say they face discouraging formal processes and procedures.

Rather than offer an open door, remove the door itself. Instead, get out there with your people and make yourself visible and available, seeking information, demanding feedback and mixing with others to hear their views and ideas. Michael Bloomberg, for example, when he became mayor of New York, implemented a 'bullpen' open-office plan, reminiscent of a Wall Street trading floor. Dozens of aides and managerial staff were seated together in a large chamber, which was intended to promote accountability and accessibility.

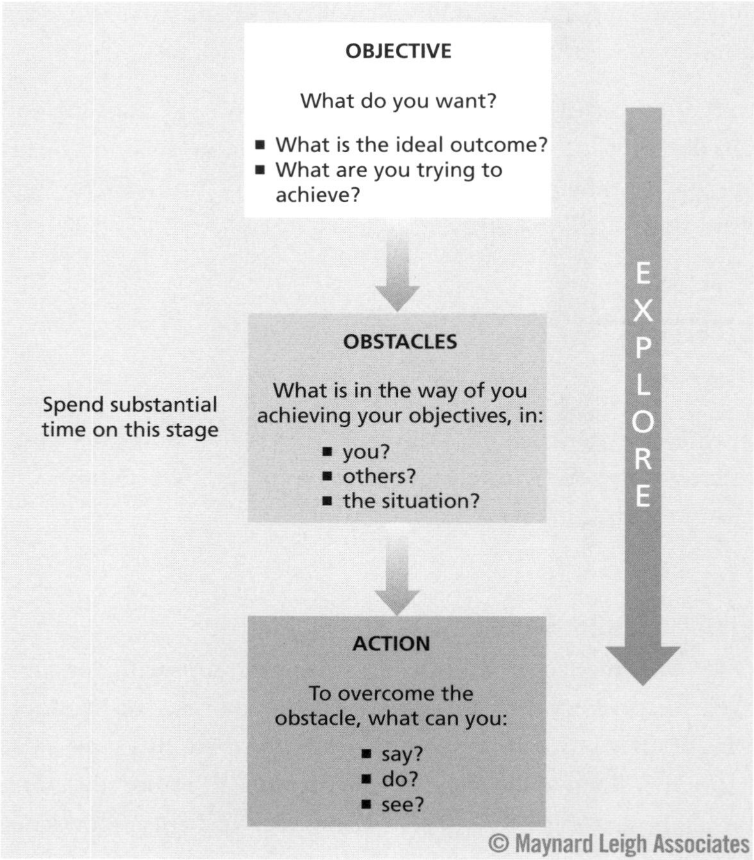

OBJECTIVE
What do you want?
What is the ideal outcome?
What are you trying to achieve?
OBSTACLES
What is in the way of you achieving your objectives, in:
you?
others?
the situation?
Spend substantial time on this stage
ACTION
To overcome the obstacle, what can you:
say?
do?
see?
EXPLORE
© Maynard Leigh Associates

Action-focused coaching

"Ask for feedback from people with diverse backgrounds. Each one will tell you one useful thing. If you're at the top of the chain, sometimes people won't give you honest feedback because they're afraid. In this case, disguise yourself, or get feedback from other sources."

Steve Jobs, founder of Apple

In Shakespeare's *Henry V*, before Agincourt the king memorably dons ordinary clothes to mix anonymously with his troops to hear what they are thinking and feeling about the coming battle. This is *leading the way* – refusing to be content with second-hand reports or hearsay, and both giving and receiving feedback.

In today's organisations many leaders are noticeably ill-equipped to deliver constructive feedback. There is often a reluctance to be direct for fear of possible conflict and damage to working relationships. Relatively few organisations have an effective performance review process. Either it has degenerated into an annual box-ticking exercise, or it is so closely tied to remuneration decisions there remains little room to explore each person's current level of engagement and involvement.

It is hardly surprising that many organisations have a culture of avoidance in tackling potentially awkward or seemingly confrontational discussions. Many top leaders do not value or pursue frank dialogue, since most people feel uncomfortable critiquing others. But this weakness can easily be overcome by a combination of the right learning and development, and repeated practice.

How to encourage people to voice their views

- Be a good listener.
- Allow the person to finish what they are saying.
- Paraphrase what you hear.
- Ask insightful, probing questions.
- Demand specifics.
- Monitor non-verbal and emotional responses.

- Express sincere thanks for even uncomfortable feedback.
- Avoid taking what you hear too personally.

If you truly want to involve people and know what's going on, start treating feedback as a gift, not a threat. This means encouraging uncomfortable or confronting information that may challenge your current perceptions of what is currently happening.

TWITTER SUMMARY

You can't lead on your own. You need to involve others. When people feel valued, involved, developed and inspired they commit to your schemes, producing greater results.

RECAP

Leading the way involves and engages everyone in what you want to achieve. It means that you identify your stakeholders, empowering them to use their full talents and ensuring they have a personal investment in achieving the result.

IDEAS FOR ACTION

✔ There are probably many different sorts of people with a stake in your success – the stakeholders. Start making a list of those who either benefit or are connected in some way with what you want to achieve.

✔ What's in it for your stakeholders to become more involved? If you can't work it out, ask them!

✔ Communicate your purpose to people.

- ✔ Ask people to join you in working towards the goal and say why you need their help. Describe how they personally can affect the outcome. Invite them to declare what they need to feel enrolled.
- ✔ Describe how the end result will affect them personally and the likely consequences of not enrolling. Set out to capture people's imagination, making them feel they will be travelling towards a worthwhile destination.
- ✔ Make meetings exciting by setting people problems. Suggest that they bring in examples of creative work from outside the business – anything to get them buzzing and involved.
- ✔ Look for new ways to give people power over their lives and their work – when people have discretion to act, there are nearly always spectacular gains in productivity.
- ✔ Show people that they are not separate from management and can help the organisation improve. In particular, demonstrate how good ideas are implemented.
- ✔ Appreciate and reward suggestions, even if they are not implemented.
- ✔ Respect people's ideas and judgement.
- ✔ Check on the personal investment your colleagues are making.
- ✔ Review whether you can reward people more for their commitment and involvement.
- ✔ Look for regular feedback on your plans and actions; ensure that your own performance is continually monitored.

05

Inspire

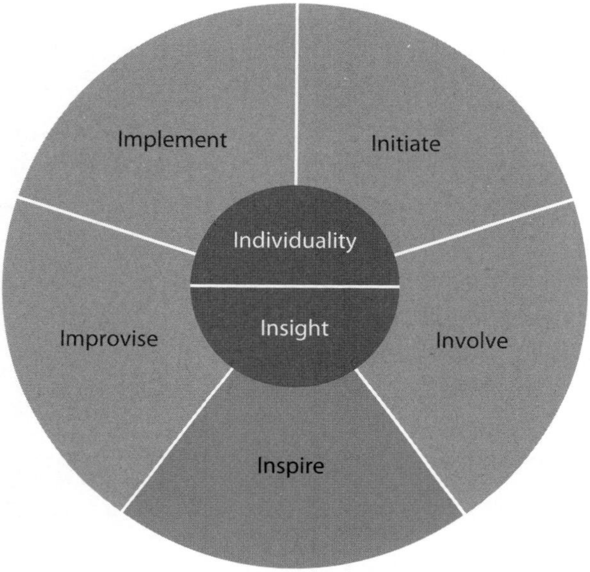

Inspiration is the one talent all leaders need to learn, claims Virgin boss Richard Branson. Given his own record, he surely knows something about how it's done.[1] We want inspiration from our leaders because it gets our juices flowing and makes us excited, keen to participate and add our own contribution. Sadly, few leaders manage to **inspire**, so it is no wonder many employees fail to perform at their best.

So what exactly do we mean by inspiration? In essence, it's a feeling – an experience that in some way moves people emotionally. This emphasis on emotion partly explains why some business leaders shy away from exploring their own potential to inspire. They fear looking too closely at their own emotions, or suffering a loss of objectivity, or becoming carried away by an irrational impulse.

[1] Richard Branson, 'The one skill leaders need to learn', Speech to SHRM 63rd Annual Conference, *Forbes*, 29 June 2011.

Inspiration tends to be seen as the preserve of artists or charismatic personalities. Yet if you have a good idea and feel strongly about it, you can be inspiring too. It's as if you have received a spark of genius from some other world. Such moments may seem totally fortuitous, but more often arrive as a result of previously intense work and preparation.

"Inspiration is a guest who doesn't like to visit lazy people."

Pyotr Ilyich Tchaikovsky, composer

Inspiration gone missing

We seldom get the inspiration we need. For instance, in a UK survey of more than 1,000 managers, most (55 per cent) said they wanted inspiration from their leaders, yet only 11 per cent said they got it.[2] A recent study by Mercer Consulting reported that over half of Britain's employees are unhappy at work and at least a third are considering leaving.

It's much the same in the US. The survey also reported that half of all US employees were unhappy. About one in three were seriously considering leaving their organisation, while another fifth viewed their employers unfavourably. 'The business consequences of this erosion in employee sentiment are significant,' claims Mercer senior partner Mindy Fox. 'Diminished loyalty and widespread apathy can undermine business performance.'[3]

Future organisations will increasingly expect their chosen leaders to be a source of inspiration. This is how they will reliably tap into

[2] Department of Trade and Industry, *Inspired Leadership: Insights into People Who Inspire Exceptional Performance*, 2004.

[3] Mercer Consulting, *What's Working*, June 2011.

the diversity and creativity of their people. Because many leaders need help in this area, there is now a UK employers' organisation dedicated to helping leaders make work experience more meaningful, relevant and inspiring for young people.[4] It responds to the gap between young people's expectation of the world of work and what business expects from new recruits.

Since you are reading a book about *leading the way*, you probably already know the need to inspire people. Yet have you taken serious time out to master how to actually do it? If you follow some of the actions outlined here and are willing to experiment, you will be able to start inspiring people on a regular basis. Leaders who inspire can generate exceptional results.

How to inspire

So how do you go about inspiring people? What does it take to move someone first to participate, then to move up the intensity levels (discussed in the last chapter) so they become fully and thrillingly engaged? Are there any sure-fire principles that trigger inspiration in others? Our advice is to take a hint from leaders who consistently inspire people. These leaders invariably rely on three learnable actions:[5]

- Saying *why* you want to achieve something, rather than what.
- Finding your own *source* of inspiration, before trying to inspire others.
- Conveying *passion* for what you want to achieve.

[4] The UK campaign 'Work Inspiration', a national employer-led campaign; www.workinspiration.com

[5] See, for example, Simon Sinek, 'How great leaders inspire action', *TED Talks*, May 2010; http://www.ted.com/talks/lang/en/simon_sinek_how_great_leaders_inspire_action.html

The why

As an inspirational leader, try to focus less on the externalities of what you want to achieve, such as 'become a market leader', 'beat the competition', 'launch breakthrough products or services', 'make money', and so on. While these envisaged destinations are really helpful when trying to communicate your vision, they are normally the external result of an internal process. Therefore, instead, your message needs to reveal what is happening inside you – what is driving the vision.

Say clearly *why* you want to achieve these things and keep explaining why it matters to you. Martin Luther King did not say 'I have a plan'. Instead, he had a dream – coming from 'inside' – and this is what inspired others.

Putting it slightly differently, people can connect at an emotional level with *why* you want to achieve something, and *why* it really matters. If they are moved by the why they start making their own transition into finding why it matters to them also, and therefore it can trigger high levels of engagement.

Sources of inspiration

The leaders who leave us touched, moved and inspired constantly examine their internal sources of inspiration. Socrates, who himself seemed pretty good at inspiring people, once proclaimed, 'The unexamined life is not worth living'. Sources of inspiration essentially come from within, even though they may be stimulated by external experiences. So, it's time to do some personal research.

What truly inspires you? What gets your juices flowing? When do you tremble with excitement? Sources of inspiration vary as much as human beings themselves. For example, inspiration might stem from a poem, a memorable film, a moving past experience, an obsession, a need for control, a hunger for making a difference, an event of great importance to you, encounters with people you admire, past successes and failures, or a cause you want to champion, such as overcoming injustice, generating enterprise or supporting the underprivileged.

You might be inspired to exceptional performance because you are facing an almost impossible, even desperate challenge. Or perhaps you want to make family members feel proud of you. Or you want to leave a lasting legacy that stamps your personal imprint on the world. All these can create an inner drive that inspires.

Sometimes the source of inspiration is an encounter with someone exceptional. For example, being in the presence of the blind and deaf Helen Keller, who was once one of the most famous women in the world, routinely reduced her visitors to tears. They felt the power of her personality and life force. Much the same is said to occur when some people have met Nelson Mandela. Or the source of inspiration may arise from an outside event, which again transforms how people feel. For example, the rescue of the Chilean miners trapped underground proved a potent source of inspiration for many people in countless endeavours around the world.

The most basic experiences can be incredibly powerful in triggering a sense of inspiration, such as the sight of a wonderful sunset, the birth of a child, a poem, or realising you are in love. In business, inspiration may stem from equally diverse sources, including particular individuals, work experiences, new opportunities, products, and so on.

"And then there is inspiration. Where does it come from? Mostly from the excitement of living. I get it from the diversity of a tree or the ripple of the sea, a bit of poetry, the sighting of a dolphin breaking the still water and moving towards me ... anything that quickens you to the instant."

Martha Graham, dancer and teacher

If you are thinking 'But nothing *does* inspire me!' do not despair. Just treat this reaction as a sign you have merely reached the starting gate. Turn your search for a source of inspiration from a task into an adventure. Never take inspiration for granted. For instance, people will not feel inspired merely because you are in a position of authority. You have to keep working at it.

People's values are also great sources of inspiration. We have looked at this in detail in Chapter 1 with regards to you as an individual, but the link with organisational values can be inspirational. There are many companies that attract the best talent because of their strong values.

Take the UK company Lush, which makes fresh handmade cosmetics. It is clearly driven by its ecological values and has a whole section on its website about what it believes. This includes the statements: 'We invent our own products and fragrances; we make them fresh by hand, using little or no preservative or packaging, using only vegetarian ingredients, and tell you when they were made. We believe in happy people making happy soap, putting our faces on our products and making our mums proud.' And when you talk to the people who work for Lush you will see how inspired they are by their company's ecological credentials.

Few people start with a blank canvas on which to develop their personal inspiration. Most of us can identify a few sources of inspiration. With a bit of thought you will soon uncover moments, things, people or experiences that caused you to feel uplifted, even if they lie buried beneath a layer of rubble and alienation. Everyone has this potential to tap into their source of inspiration – you just have to keep at it. But don't expect to be able to inspire others unless you can first find inspiration for yourself.

Passion

Almost without exception, leaders who inspire people exude a passion that moves people. Having found their own source of inspiration, they are almost unstoppable in wanting to tell others about it. They are willing to make themselves vulnerable in showing what they truly care about. They risk rejection, ridicule and misunderstanding.

If 'passion' makes you uncomfortable, try 'commitment' or perhaps 'conviction'. Whatever the semantics, in essence can you talk with energy, enthusiasm and strong emotion about what you want to achieve? You will not succeed if you rely on a logical and apparently watertight case. What moves people are not facts and figures, graphs or tables, tight reasoning or pure information. What inspires people is when you share your energy, enthusiasm and strength of feeling for some course of action you care about. People need to fully grasp why it matters so much to you.

As a leadership tool for inspiring people, passion is often misunderstood. It is interpreted as ranting and excessive emotional outbursts, which set many people's teeth on edge. In politicians this becomes demagoguery. In contrast, leadership passion that really works is when you emotionally connect to what you want to happen and speak from the heart. You might speak softly, gently or quietly; but you will have a grounded and compelling intensity. This kind of personal connection almost always comes across as convincing and starts to engage other people's emotions too.

Benefits from using passion

For leaders, passion can:

- provide direction and focus
- create energy
- foster creativity
- heighten personal performance
- inspire action – yours and others'

- attract employees and customers
- build loyalty
- provide a distinctive edge
- take the organisation to a higher plane.

We are referring to purposeful passion, not wild abandon. Passion used well is full of direction, concentrated like a laser beam, slicing through objections, obstacles, inertia and negativity. When you find your passion, you will have located a source of immense power. The bad news is that it cannot be faked; people soon know when your passion is forced.

Passionate leaders are not afraid to let their feelings show. This does not mean being reduced to a tearful mess, though more than one leader has allowed tears to flow in the passion of the moment. If you seek to inspire people as a leader, do not fear passion, but rather fear its absence. When you express how strongly you feel about something, it can transform how people view you and begin to move them from perhaps cool scepticism to warm enthusiasm.

Vision

"The single defining quality of leaders is the capacity to create and realise a vision."

Warren Bennis, scholar, organisational consultant and author

Vision is an important part of creating inspiration in others and separates leaders from non-leaders. It involves being able to imagine a better future. You envision that future in your mind's eye. By creating a compelling picture of the future you can talk about it with passion. It should be a bold prospect – something that makes people excited when you describe it. Nor can you stop there. Importantly, let each person know *how* they can contribute to turning your vision into a reality.

Sometimes a leader's vision comes in disguise. For example, when Lou Gerstner was parachuted in to rescue IBM he famously declared that the last thing it needed right then was a vision. But that did not stop him pursuing what was indeed a vision: transforming IBM from a computer company to a technology and services company in which the internet played a key role.

A powerful personal vision usually differs from those will-o'-the-wisp statements that permeate so many mission statements adorning corporate walls. If your vision is to be more than just a 'nice to have', somehow you must bring it alive for people. Research shows that only 3 per cent of the typical business leader's time is spent envisioning and winning people's commitment to their vision.[6] *Leading the way* demands that you not merely have a vision but that you have one that you can share with others – so that they come to own it too. A shared vision does not happen with merely a 3 per cent investment.

When it comes to vision there is seldom a miracle moment, rather it's a daily journey. It's a journey that requires constant investment in modelling the right behaviours, and in communication and the management of people's expectations.

Your colleagues can help you identify your vision, expand it and translate it into a universal message. For example, FedEx's famous three-word vision is 'People, Service, Profit'. By themselves these words are useless and may as well stay where they belong in some mundane dictionary. FedEx leaders, though, have turned them

[6] James Kouzes and Barry Posner, 'To lead, create a shared vision', *Harvard Business Review*, January 2009.

into a reality so they now drive the company's day-to-day working. But it took considerable time and much mutual help to evolve.

Your vision as a leader can be strategic, tactical or personal.

- **Strategic vision** is long-term and describes how the world would look if you could somehow eliminate all obstacles and achieve what you want. If you are a senior leader, this is likely to be an overriding philosophy and provide a framework into which all activities fit. For example, Google's strategic vision is to help organise the world's information; and the vision of Brazil's energy company Petrobras for 2020 includes the goal of becoming the preferred company among its areas of public interest. Even if you are not a CEO you can still have such a vision: simply apply it to your local sphere of influence.
- **Tactical vision** drives short-term action and provides people with clear guidance on what to do in different situations. It is best if you can evolve this with those you want to make this vision come alive. For example, your tactical vision might be to sell more products and services, expand market share domestically and overseas, retain enough cash to sustain long-term profitability, or create an office environment that truly expresses your culture.
- **Personal vision** is your own view of yourself – how you want to be. This might be an aspiration, or some state of being you are reaching for, rather than one already acquired. For example, you might have a vision to build a powerful personal network, raise your profile within your industry, make a major creative contribution in improving health care, be known as influential in your sphere of interest, or build a company that makes a difference to how people spend their time at work.

Whatever the vision, it must really matter to you – no half measures. Unless it is important to you, it will never convince or inspire others. One way of tapping into your vision is to start with your own values – your core beliefs that seldom alter.

Many who aspire to be leaders complain that because the top team does not seem to have a vision, therefore they cannot have one either. This is a narrow view of what vision offers. All visions operate within constraints. It is like saying that because you cannot decide how the world will be in the future, you cannot picture how your home could be improved. You just need a bit of imagination.

"Imagination is like a muscle. If you don't exercise it, it goes to seed."

Joan Littlewood, theatre director

Ten key questions about your vision

1. How much effort are you investing in developing a shared vision?
2. How much time are you spending in winning commitment?
3. Can you describe your vision in less than one minute?
4. What is it about your vision that excites you, or moves you in some way?
5. Why is your vision important to you?
6. Are you constantly sharing interesting stories, anecdotes and events that illustrate your vision?
7. What big questions does your vision address?
8. Does your vision offer a dream beyond what people currently think is possible?
9. How would things look if your vision became a reality?
10. What will your legacy be in ten years' time?

Vision acts as a force within – compelling you to action. It can give you a clear sense of purpose. And the power of the vision and your devotion to it can inspire others. They will sense your resolve and commitment.

Communication

> "Communication is talking *with* people, not *at* them. And when you talk *at* people you do not get execution."
>
> **Allan Leighton, chairman of Pace and former CEO of Asda**

In late 2010, Marc Bolland, the new CEO of Marks & Spencer, revealed his long-awaited vision for making the stores more inspirational and how he would dismantle many of the strategies put in place by his predecessor. Spelling it out in more detail, he explained he wanted to concentrate on improving UK stores by focusing on the clothing, home and food businesses.

Bolland's vision would be useless locked inside his head. If you truly care about how the future should look you will be driven, like Bolland at M&S, to share it with others. Around the time you become sick of talking about your vision, people will just start to get it. Communication is a continuous process, a constant drip, drip of the same messages until they finally land. For example, can your team repeat back your vision or values for what drives the team? If you dropped in to see them, would they explain it with words that roughly match yours?

Tomorrow's organisations will rely heavily for their success on building relationships, seeking collaboration and working across organisational boundaries. This implies a demand for leaders who can support these complex requirements by communicating vision in compelling ways. Do you need to hone your skills of influencing, persuasion and story telling? Are you familiar with techniques to support your message?

Communication tips

- **Clear purpose**. Be clear about your intention. What are you trying to achieve with your communication? As a result of it, what should people be thinking? How do you want them to feel? What do you want them to do differently?
- **Emotion**. Inject into your messages an emotional content that clearly moves you and is therefore likely to move others.
- **Visual imagery**. Use pictures to stimulate the part of the brain that works by instinct, feeling and non-verbal concepts. You may not even need an actual picture. For example, Bill Gates' word picture 'We want to put a computer on every desk and home in the world' created a memorable mental image.
- **Clarity and succinctness**. Make sure your messages are crystal clear and not woolly or full of waffle. See if you can sum up your ideas as an 'elevator pitch', then as a headline in a newspaper.
- **Metaphors**. Add metaphors to inject life and energy into your vision message. Metaphors can have more impact than simple explanations. For example, when campaigners against genetically modified foods started to talk about Frankenstein foods, they started to have more impact.
- **Charisma**. Use your personality, confidence and relationship skills to give added impact to your message.
- **Focus on your audience**. Always have your attention on the people you are speaking to – are they attentive, do they understand what you're saying, do you need to speed up or slow down?

Conversation

As a leader you may be tempted to think that you need to do all the communicating yourself. It is certainly true that you will have to do a lot, and when you do present or communicate it needs to be compelling and memorable. However, given that leadership is relational, most of your communication will be a dialogue rather than a monologue. By promoting discussion and allowing people to explore your messages for themselves, they are more likely to become inspired.

Any communication strategy you devise should include tactics to encourage conversation. You want to get people talking. It is interesting to note how rumours spread round organisations. They spread fast because they address people at their own level of interest and they tend to be quite intimate – hence the phrase 'whispering campaigns'. If you can spread your own ideas in this way, you are more likely to produce engagement.

Story-telling

"The best stories enthuse wonder."

Andrew Stanton, film director and screenwriter

We have all been brought up on stories that captivated us as children. They are a natural form of communication and therefore a powerful mechanism for getting our messages across. There is a story in every situation you find yourself in. And that applies to your vision of the future as well. What is the story you want to tell about the changes you want to make? Can you paint a mental picture of what the improved condition will look like? Is your current business story compelling enough to inspire people? If not, what can you create instead?

And the same goes for the legends that are told within organisations. People will always have a tendency to tell stories about their workplace, so you might as well try to harness this tendency and create the narrative yourself. Think about the stories you would like people to spread.

Some company stories have become legends that embody the spirit of the organisation – for instance, the story about the setting up of Innocent Drinks. The founders, Richard Reed, Adam Balon and Jon Wright, tell the tale:

> We started Innocent in 1999 after selling our smoothies at a music festival. We put up a big sign asking people if they thought we should give up our jobs to make smoothies, and put a bin saying 'Yes' and a bin saying 'No' in front of the stall. Then we got people to vote with their empties. At the end of the weekend, the 'Yes' bin was full, so we resigned from our jobs the next day and got cracking.'[7]

Trust

No matter how compelling your vision or how strongly or passionately you communicate your ideas and plans, they will only start to inspire people once those people trust you. Their unspoken question, and sometimes one that is actually voiced, is 'Why should we believe you will make this initiative happen?'

To answer this requires you have to have a manifest faith in yourself. When people see you trust yourself, this self-belief soon communicates and can engender trust in others. The unspoken answer then becomes 'If you believe it will happen, then maybe we should too.'

"You have got to discover you, what you do and trust it"

Barbara Streisand

[7] www.innocentdrinks.co.uk/us/our-story

Building trust is seldom a quick fix and nearly always a two-way affair. If you can't trust them, why should they trust you? For example, how far do you trust people who work with you? Are you constantly checking on their progress, frequently asking them to explain their actions, or demanding they clear all decisions with you, regardless of how important or urgent the decisions are?

If you want to get ordinary people to do extraordinary things, you need to win their trust first. That's inspirational. One method is to hold a view of people that is greater than the view they have of themselves. You entrust them with tasks and responsibilities that help them grow and develop, and you let them know you believe in them.

> "Treat people as if they were what they ought to be, and you'll help them to become what they are capable of becoming."
>
> **Johann Wolfgang von Goethe, writer and polymath**

Challenging goals

Setting great goals is like finalising the decision to become an amazing person. This is why leaders attach so much importance to goal setting. It is how they unlock people's potential to excel. In Chapter 7 we will look at the process of goal setting in more detail. Yet the essence of inspiring goals, whether a leader sets them or the person sets them for themselves, is that they are exciting challenges.

Sadly, goal setting is often seen purely as a mechanism for driving people to extra effort, and then further discredited by the notion that as soon as you achieve a target 'they move the goal-posts!' That is why goals need to be collaborative as well as inspiring.

When done with the right spirit, they can be a fantastic way of galvanising people's energy. You only need to look at some of the extraordinary endeavours that have been sparked by almost impossible goals, whether it be putting a human being on the Moon, building the Hadron Collider or curing malaria in Africa.

TWITTER SUMMARY

Leaders don't motivate, they inspire. By being inspired themselves, they are infectious in communicating their vision for a better future.

RECAP

Inspirational leadership moves people in some way so that they feel differently and become willing to do unusual things. Leaders who inspire share their vision, are great communicators, have a real passion about their beliefs, and excite people to join them to go in the right direction.

IDEAS FOR ACTION

- ✔ Spend time exploring the sources of your own inspiration; for example, immerse yourself in what seems to get you excited, moves you, or makes you feel uplifted.
- ✔ Discuss with your team what inspires them – discover what inspires other people around you.
- ✔ Make a list of events, poems, works of art, films, books, people, plays, scenery and so on that uplift you in some way.
- ✔ Involve others in your idea of vision and what it means to you. Together, work at articulating a vision and how it could be made meaningful in the workplace.

- ✔ Tap into your own or your team's vision by exploring values – those core beliefs that you and they feel strongly about. Try determining these by answering the question: 'What really matters to me (us) is …'
- ✔ Try turning the mental picture of what you want into a simple drawing – a quick sketch, diagram, cartoon or whatever; it doesn't matter if you are a poor artist, just let the drawing speak for itself.
- ✔ Find specific, practical examples to explain and firm up your vision; keep your messages short and convey simply the results you want.
- ✔ Show personal commitment by talking about your vision.
- ✔ Be active in creating new ways of explaining your leadership message.
- ✔ Listen to what others have to say about the vision to help to refine it. See how this makes you clearer and able to communicate it more effectively.
- ✔ Be willing to talk passionately about what you want to achieve; never try to fake it – people soon realise when it's forced.
- ✔ Remember that passionate leaders allow their feelings to show – you move others when you are willing to be moved yourself.
- ✔ Try to really excite people about where you want to take them; if you aren't excited by the destination, why should they be?
- ✔ Encourage the selection of challenging goals that demand people do more than just be average.

06

Improvise

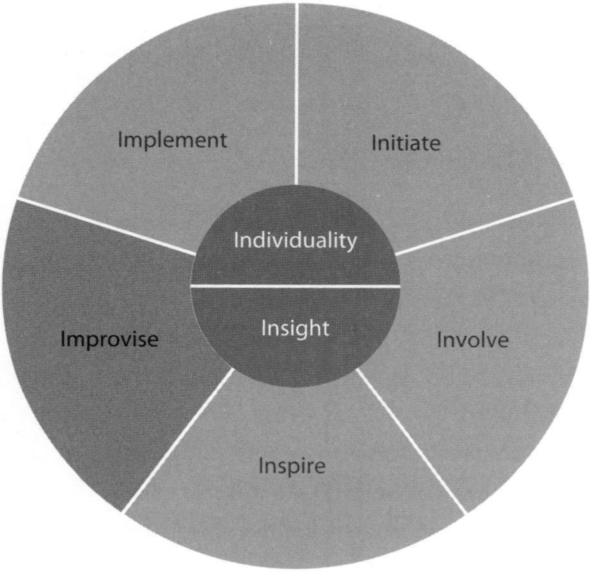

Asked about his plan for getting out of trouble, the movie hero Indiana Jones replies 'I don't know, I'm just making it up as I go along'. It's what many successful leaders also do in running their organisations. The ability to **improvise**, be adaptable and find unexpected solutions will make you particularly valuable as a leader in organisations in the twenty-first century.

If you want to make God laugh, goes one reliable aphorism, 'Tell her your plans'. Regardless, conventional executives devote serious time and energy trying to remove uncertainty about what is over the horizon. In practice, the future continues its never-ending ability to spring surprises. If you *lead the way* you will fully realise this. Your answer will be to adjust, change direction, adapt and constantly seek creative solutions. This commitment to improvising is strength not weakness. It realises that just because something worked last time, there is no guarantee that it will work again.

Describing strategy, for example, the renowned leadership guru Rosabeth Moss Kanter uses a compelling simile. 'It's like improvisational theatre', she argues. 'The players must be willing to take on unfamiliar roles, think on their feet, pay attention to several things at once, walk into situations for which they are not prepared.'[1]

The drive for improvisation

Consider what most of tomorrow's companies will be facing. On the one hand will be constant uncertainty, risk and paradox. On the other, in the cause of faster responses to deal with what the future throws at them, will be pressure to network, collaborate and reduce hierarchies. So, you will need to become skilful at rapidly adapting and playing it by ear. This will be true whether dealing with strategy, making decisions about new products, agreeing a marketing campaign or helping a team in trouble. In some places this is now the default way of getting things done, solving problems, winning engagement and generating innovation.

In such an environment, relying on issuing instructions or automatically expecting obedience or even attention is doomed. To succeed, your leadership must tap into the creative benefits of diversity, ever-expanding networks and constant collaboration that will undermine or subvert hierarchies and formal lines of control.

> "Our emerging workforce is not interested in command and control leadership. They don't want to do things because I said so; they want to do things because they want to do them. The captain of industry who continues to run his business in a militaristic, siloed way cannot compete in this global economy."
>
> **Irene Rosenfeld, CEO of Kraft Foods**

[1] R. Kanter, 'Strategy as improvisational theater', *MIT Sloan Management Review*, 43 (2), 2002.

In times like these, the clear requirement will be greater tolerance of risk than in the past. Once, being risk-averse won plaudits. Looking ahead though, handling uncertainty and risk will partly define the nature of progressive organisations. It means responding far more flexibly than in the past.

Our own company, Maynard Leigh, has pioneered the use of theatre techniques in management development, so it should be no surprise that we draw on our own experience of improvising in the performance arts for ideas about tackling uncertainty. For instance, frequently treating risk as an opportunity for creativity and innovation is behaving rather like a great stage performer – as outlined in the box.

Improvising creatively

Great stage performers and improvising leaders say:

- I trust that I can do it.
- I have permission to experiment and play.
- Risk involves failure.
- Things going wrong will be part of the process – I will be creative with failure.
- Stop being obstructive and allow my natural talent to perform.
- I will listen hard and learn what I must do.
- I will be 'in the moment' – it just went!
- A strong form and structure gives me flexibility.
- Practise, practise, practise.
- Yes to colleagues' offerings – I'll work with what they give me.

▶

- I accept no immutable rules, only approximations and guidelines.
- I am not alone – I will collaborate.

For 40 years, the renowned film and stage director Mike Leigh has employed his own particular method of devising plays and movies using improvisation. Along the way he has gathered plenty of praise and prizes. His approach has important lessons for *leading the way*, since leading organisations can be just as messy as theatrical improvisation. 'First, the actors take part without any idea of the process,' he says. 'Second, each actor only knows what his character would know.' The rest is created through interaction and creativity. As a leader you will only know your part, not what everyone else can do. Finding out is part of improvising.

> "Don't ever think you've arrived, and remember that what you don't know is so much more than what you do."
>
> **Indra Nooyi, CEO of PepsiCo**

Leadership improvisation is doing something that has not previously been done. For instance Karen Bradley, chief executive of West Ham United, became the first woman to run a top-flight football club, Birmingham City. When it floated in 1997, she became the youngest managing director of a UK public company. 'No one had thought of football as an industry before,' she says. 'The business of football hadn't been fully explored and its ability to build relationships.'[2]

And when the creator of FedEx based the delivery company's approach around a wheel and spoke principle, he was improvising.

[2] P. Whitehead, 'Superwoman? It's absolute bull', *Financial Times*, 15 March 2012.

He did not know for sure it would work. Many in the industry who knew the concept had previously dismissed it. Yet it worked, as today's vast number of FedEx vans, planes, ships, boxes and hub-centres shows.

How improvising helps leadership performance

- Presence – being fully in the moment, listening, and paying attention.
- Thinking on your feet – responding confidently in the moment while under pressure.
- Real-time adapting – adapting strategy as new information and situations emerge.
- Discovery – finding new and surprising solutions to old and new situations.
- Resourcefulness – recognising and using the unexpected as an opportunity.
- Resilience – bouncing back quickly after 'failures' or dead ends.
- Impactfulness – encouraging risk-taking and spontaneous behaviours from others.
- Influence – getting buy-in and support for your initiatives.
- 'Ours' thinking – fostering team-thinking in terms of 'Look what *we* did!'
- Taking action – applying techniques to improve systems, products and processes.

Source: Adapted from The Center for Creative Emergence, www.creativeemergence.com, reproduced with permission.

Improvisation in organisations is now a vibrant area of study, moving from a marginal activity to mainstream.[3] Many traditional businesses are bringing in comic improvisers and theatre practitioners to work with their managers in order to improve their ability to create spontaneously and respond flexibly to change. And even those peddlers of management science, the business schools, realise they can hardly sound convincing on how to lead unless they acknowledge the increasing role of improvisation. For example, MIT Sloane School of Management has launched a course applying it to leadership. Students practise improvisation techniques and then apply these concepts to business situations.

"The improvisational model throws out the script, brings in the audience, and trusts the actors to be unpredictable – that is, to innovate."

Rosabeth Moss Kanter, Professor of Business Administration, Harvard Business School

Principles of improvisation

The notion of creating something out of nothing may sound like a recipe for undisciplined chaos, and suggest that anything that is created is a matter of chance. The opposite is true. Underlying the apparent messiness is a set of principles that improvisers in the performing arts use all the time. Jazz musicians, for instance, will use keys and chord structures as the basis for their improvised embellishments. It is these underlying structures that give performers the freedom to let go. It is a very disciplined process.

[3] See, for example, M.P. Cunha, K. Kamoche and R. Cunha, 'Organizational improvisation and leadership', *International Studies of Management and Organization*, **33** (1), 2003.

So, what are the underlying principles governing acting improvisation, which can be applied to organisation life? Here are three of them:

1 **Accept and build**. This means you behave in a 'Yes, and . . .' way. You accept other people's ideas and suggestions and add value to them. 'Yes, and . . .' assumes creative potential, where alternatives, contradictions and paradoxes are embraced, because they are often the source and stimulus of invention. If you can hear another team member's contribution as an offering that might allow you to create something of value, then you remove the impulse to kill it off. You can accept it for what it is, without having to criticise it, and instead just build on it. See if you can say 'Yes' to ideas and comments made by colleagues and create with them. That way, you value their input and see it as an opportunity. And it is more likely that you will then invent something quite unexpected. It's the best route towards what people often refer to as 'out of the box' thinking.

Dealing with 'Yes, but . . .'

If you are dealing with people who habitually respond with 'Yes, but . . .' (rather than 'Yes, and . . .'), there are various tactics that you could try:

- **What's really going on?** Understand where their reservations are coming from. Really try to address their needs and concerns.
- **Make them aware**. Point out their habit of saying 'Yes, but . . .', rather than 'Yes, and . . .'. Do they know they're doing it?
- **Impact**. Tell them how it makes you feel. What is the potentially demoralising effect their response has on you and others?
- **Give up**. Simply say, 'Oh, OK, I won't do anything then', and see how they react.

▶

- **Ask for alternatives**. Rather than trying to further defend your idea in the face of their opposition, ask for their suggestions. In other words, try to get them to turn their 'Yes, but ...' into a constructive suggestion.
- **'Yes, but ...' back**. No, not tit for tat, but a way to try building on their objections and working creatively with them.

2 **Make the other person succeed**. Actors improvising on stage know how exposing and humiliating it is if something they do does not work. Therefore, they are totally dependent on their colleagues for support – during their performance the actors are interdependent. This is sometimes not the case in organisations. Often so-called teams are actually groups with conflicting interests – for instance, sales teams may have bonuses that depend on their individual success. So, first of all, seek areas where your team members depend on each other to deliver results. And if there isn't an area, create one – for example, ask the team for suggestions about how to raise performance, or how to make the company a great place to work. If each person is committed to the success of others, then there is mutual benefit and the chance to become more than the sum of the parts. This approach is also essential in the new world of collaborative working. Often competitor companies have to work together on projects. If they can learn to improvise together, they stand a better chance of success.

3 **Take risks**. We have already talked about the need to be risky if you are *leading the way*. It is particularly true when improvising. You are stepping out into the unknown, into uncharted territory. That's what it takes to be creative. And this is where the two principles above can support you. They encourage people to work together by committing to each other and by accepting and building on each other's ideas. You can lead the process and yet are part of it as well. It may be a bit scary, but you are not alone.

Although we can identify certain principles of improvisation, much of it depends on trusting instinct or gut feel. Leadership improvising also focuses on three key areas:

- creativity
- flexibility
- presence.

Creativity

When organisations consider creativity, many regard it as strictly the territory for artists or confined to narrow areas like new product development or marketing campaigns. They even refer to 'the creatives' as if they are a different breed of employee, with their own peculiar behaviours. *Leading the way* means you understand and relish creativity far more broadly. You see and welcome it as relevant just about anywhere – in relationships, systems, processes, environments, and so on.

As a leader it's your job to harness the creative energy that lies within your immediate sphere of influence – and even beyond it. There are numerous ways to do this, including encouraging innovation, establishing a 'try it' environment, problem solving, ensuring people's ideas are valued, and embracing the whole idea of play. Whatever way you choose, you will require a clear understanding of how the creative process works and know how to encourage it.

Understanding the creative process

1 **Preparation**. First, those involved become immersed in the problem at an information-gathering stage. When it's a team effort there is the formation of roles, areas of special individual interest and coordination of tasks.

▶

2 **Frustration**. Coming up with new ideas and solutions can be a difficult process. Most creative endeavours involve a period of aggravation as you grope around in the unknown. Be patient, it's all part of the process.

3 **Incubation**. This stage allows time for reflection, and for the unconscious to work. The immediate problem may seem on the back burner, forgotten or neglected. But minds are still working. For a team, it can mean not meeting for a while, allowing thinking time and time to have ideas.

4 **Illumination**. This is the 'Aha' or 'Eureka' moment when ideas or innovations surface without warning. There is seldom an immediate 'killer insight', but some new angle may occur. With a team, sometimes you only need to bring everyone together again for ideas to surface.

5 **Execution**. This final stage separates mere creativity from successful innovation. New ideas require action, stubborn persistence and an ability to build support for change. Perhaps more than anything else, execution takes courage and persistence.

Innovation

"When you innovate you've got to be prepared for everyone telling you you're nuts."

Harry Ellison, co-founder and CEO of Oracle

Innovation turns improvisation into tangible results. Even if you don't see yourself as a particularly creative person, you will need to know how to encourage this process by legitimising a culture in which others feel able to innovate.

For instance, Google is famous for its informal '20 per cent time' initiative. Under this system, Google employees are free to devote about one day per week to a project they feel passionate about, regardless of whether it relates to their usual job duties. These initiatives are then filtered and new ideas selected to be pursued.

Paul Clarke, director of technology for Ocado, is similarly well aware of the need to constantly break new ground in terms of IT, as well as keeping his team of extremely bright people engaged. So he has put in place various initiatives to encourage creativity. For instance, he has established a bottom-up forum for developers to propose a new idea and get the support they need to develop it to the point where it can be decided if it has legs; a sort of 'Dragon's Den' style of internal venture capital fund. He also fosters a spirit of healthy competition by organising 'hackathons' and other such technical contests.

Supporting innovation also means tackling obstacles to it. For instance, you may need to put your head above the parapet and challenge existing processes and systems that inhibit people's freedom to create. This can be uncomfortable, and you really have to believe in what generates innovation to do this. For example, many companies claim to value creativity and innovation, yet are locked into restrictive practices that discourage fresh thinking, punish failure and reduce the chance of generating breakthroughs.

In creating a drive to innovate, people are far more important than processes, money, research or structures. That is why leadership plays such a crucial role in ensuring the right climate exists in which innovation can occur.

How to promote innovation

- Change the surroundings to encourage fresh thinking.
- Brainstorm with open-ended questions.
- Reward new ideas.
- Encourage thinking time.
- Have times when the team simply has fun.
- Remove communication barriers between team members and management.
- Discuss the current culture and how changes can impact the organisation's culture.
- Be accessible – encourage team members to share new ideas more often.
- Welcome diversity of thoughts and opinions.
- Set innovation goals, such as 'Redo the entire website by year end'.
- Select the most promising innovators, and encourage the unexpected.
- Create 'buffer zones' for the most innovative people.
- Give innovators room to 'play'.
- Resist the temptation to look for immediate results.
- Commit to driving the best ideas through to implementation.

A 'try it' environment

Sheryl Sandberg, a 37-year old vice-president, made a mistake that cost Google several million dollars. When she informed the founder Larry Page, he replied, 'I'm so glad you made this mistake, because I want to run a company where we are moving too quickly and doing too much, not being too cautious and doing too little. If we don't have any of these mistakes, we're just not taking enough risks.'[4]

To really encourage a creative approach to improvisation you need to ensure you encourage a 'try it' environment. This is one where mistakes may not be welcomed, but are not punished either. In the case of Google, Page saw the expensive mistake as an important learning experience. Mistakes are part of any learning process and should be acceptable – within agreed limits. That's the ideal. In practice it's a hard freedom for some organisations to tolerate. Some never make the necessary switch to a culture that resists punishing mistakes. They find it impossible to remain non-judgemental, or to keep asking: 'What did we learn from that?' As a leader you can help promote that shift by how you treat mistakes.

Organisations hoping to raise production standards often set high quality standards that promote fault-free actions. While commendably disciplined, the result can also close off 'try it' opportunities, leading to even worse problems. Toyota recognised this danger when it allowed any worker on the production line the freedom to act if they saw something going wrong. This led to far higher quality standards than previous attempts to impose quality through post-production inspectors and the like. Other companies arrived at a similar conclusion, regularly turning mistakes and errors into positive learning experiences.

Vicki Updike, president at Miles Kimball, a US direct-marketing company, describes the firm's 'ask me' suggestion scheme. 'If someone has an idea, our attitude is "Let's try it".' She continues: 'We are very proud of our employees ... We are not the kind of company that will spend time criticizing what will not work. We learn and we move on.'[5]

[4] J. Kouzes and B. Posner, *The Leadership Challenge*, Jossey-Bass, 2007.

[5] Sean Johnson, 'Miles Kimball empowers employees', *Insight*, 1 January 2011.

Seven things failure is not

1 Failure is not avoidable – sooner or later, human beings are bound to fail.
2 Failure is not an event, but a process – success is simply a journey.
3 Failure is not objective – only the person involved can say for sure it's a failure.
4 Failure is not the enemy – it takes adversity to achieve success; it is a fertiliser.
5 Failure is not irreversible – all situations have some potential for recovery.
6 Failure is not a stigma – it is not a permanent marker, merely a step towards success.
7 Failure is not final – it is simply a price to pay to achieve success.

In a 'try it' environment the only unacceptable risks are those that damage people or 'hole the ship below the waterline', that is, put the entire enterprise at risk.

"If I had to live my life again, I'd make the same mistakes, only sooner."

Tullulah Bankhead, actress

When you say to people 'Let's try it' you are giving them the freedom to make mistakes and learn, not a licence to be reckless. In such an environment you do not ignore mistakes by simply shrugging your shoulders and saying 'That's too bad'. As a leader you grab these mistakes and use them as an opportunity to encourage yet more learning – to get it right next time and to build improved systems.

Problem-solve

Much of your work as a leader is likely to be about solving problems. The more interesting the problem, the more absorbing the work becomes. The most difficult problems will inevitably tend to gravitate towards you to resolve. You will have few precedents to guide a decision and instead need a creative response involving flair, instinct, the ability to improvise and judgement. After all, you're a leader – you're there to use your judgement.

Take, for example, emerging markets. For most leaders these represent an obvious opportunity, and where much of their attention may well be directed. Yet a leader with a flair to improvise may see the problem entirely differently: 'For me, the biggest emerging market isn't a country, it's women. We have 600 million people living on a dollar a day and two-thirds of those beneath the poverty line are women.' No, this is not some head of an international charity, but Andrea Jung, CEO of Avon Products, the world's largest direct seller operating in more than 120 countries.[6]

If you're *leading the way*, you need to spend less time worrying and focus instead on seeking solutions to important problems rather than what is not working. For example, with sliding revenues in a digital age and the printed page no longer core business, the big problem at Xerox was how to redefine the company's entire purpose. Ursula Burns, the first African-American woman to lead a top-100 US corporation, tackled the problem and improvised a bold solution. With a dramatic $6.4 billion acquisition of ACS, the IT outsourcing service company, she solved Xerox's problem by turning it into a global leader in document management and business processes.

[6] *Financial Times*, 'Women at the top', 16 November 2011.

You may not be able to spend billions to solve a problem like Burns at Xerox, but you can develop your approach to improvising solutions. For example, imagine how things could be if you simply had a magic wand; or think how someone you really admire would approach the problem; or see the problem as if it were a useful part of your situation; or brainstorm ideas for making the problem much worse!

The SCAMPER technique

When tackling difficult problems, you could try asking the following questions:

- **S** What could you **S**ubstitute for the current product/service/factor?
- **C** How could you **C**ombine different elements to produce something new?
- **A** How could you **A**dapt current processes or products to create something different?
- **M** What if you **M**agnify, **M**inimise or **M**odify what you've already got?
- **P** How could you **P**ut your skills/product/services to other uses?
- **E** What would happen if you **E**liminated certain aspects?
- **R** How could you **R**everse or **R**e-align what is currently happening?

When looking for solutions, leaders will often resort to unusual methods – anything to get a fresh perspective. For example, you might encourage people to draw the problem as a picture, a symbol or a cartoon. That way they access a part of their brain that does not think logically, but visually and holistically. Or set up a playful situation where colleagues see a problem in new ways. For example, a senior engineer in Rolls Royce, returning from a trip abroad, called his team together and placed a sophisticated Japanese camera on the table. 'If we had to build this at Rolls Royce,' he asked, 'what would it cost?' When the group produced its answer and compared it with the Japanese price, everyone was shocked at the difference. It prompted major new thinking about engine production methods.

Value ideas

In Chapter 4 we referred to the ITV engagement process that elicited 9,000 suggestions and how the leadership followed up on the ideas. It is important that you demonstrate how much you value people's contribution. US utility Xcel Energy wanted to reward its rank-and-file for taking the initiative, so it created 'Xpress Ideas', a rewards scheme that paid bonuses on the spot for useful submissions. The programme was a hit among the company's 11,000 people and in one year they offered 6,133 suggestions, most of which were implemented. If there is a single golden guideline for rewarding ideas it is: celebrate the *person* not the idea. People relate to people, and if you receive great suggestions then make sure you put those who contribute centre stage.

When improvising, you are seeking a state of 'flow' – when creative ideas are surging forward. You need to have systems in place that quickly move any viable new idea from its source to where it's needed. Suggestion boxes, emails, networks and other open systems can process ideas, but you will need to ensure there is a constant stream of ideas flowing through your organisation. And your people need to know that you take creativity seriously.

Seven ways to deter new ideas

Poor leaders kill off creativity in a number of ways. Here's how they do it:

1 Make idea givers go through lots of hoops before submission.

▶

2 Insist suggestions must lead to big organisational returns – ignoring the fact that it's the accumulation of many small ideas that normally adds up to major gains.

3 Refuse to offer a tangible reward for the effort.

4 Apparently welcome suggestions, then qualify with 'Yes but …'

6 Always refer to the past: 'We tried that in …', 'When we did that last time, it …'.

7 Denigrate those making suggestions: 'What do you know about it?'; 'You don't have the full picture'.

Encourage play

"I think fun should be a motivator for all business. We've been successful because we've done things differently, and that's made life more fun and enjoyable."

Richard Branson, founder of Virgin

People perform at their best when fully engaged and the atmosphere is playful. An enlivened workplace tends to promote creativity and innovation. Research by psychologists shows that individuals produce more creative solutions for everyday problems in a playful rather than a serious atmosphere. A culture of play not only brings a workplace alive, it generates 'meaning' and makes people keen to turn up each day. Just look at the energy that is often released when people take part in Comic Relief fundraising events. Raising money for good causes is a desperately serious business, yet look at the fun people have doing it.

The corporate world started taking the idea of play seriously when business consultant Pat Kane coined the phrase 'the play ethic' in response to the accepted notion of the work ethic. Others have built on this idea. For example, the LEGO Group created a playful experiential process designed to enhance innovation and business performance. It was based on research that shows hands-on, minds-on learning produces a deeper, more meaningful understanding of the world and its possibilities. Many other major organisations have also experimented with this approach.

How do you promote serious play to help you improvise as a leader? Here are some approaches you can try:

- **Prototyping**. Create a first version of a new idea, such as a new product; your prototype is successful if people make useful suggestions for how to improve it.
- **Environment**. Create a play space with colour and craft materials so that people can express ideas in visual ways and simply feel free to experiment.
- **Games**. Encourage people to play both competitive and collaborative games, so they find solutions in a lively environment and generate new perspectives.
- **Fun projects**. Set up tasks or challenges outside the work scene that indirectly relate to the issues you are dealing with – for example, help a charity solve a similar issue.
- **Simulations**. Devise situations that allow people to experience a different reality; for example, handling a sudden crisis, responding to a price war, handling a takeover.
- **Forum theatre**. Use actors to bring alive a work issue and invite colleagues to interact with them to try out different responses or courses of action.
- **Brainstorming**. Make your brainstorming sessions fun by having music playing, or provide sweets and treats, or run them in an unusual location.

- **Laughter**. Establish a playful environment where people can readily laugh together and enjoy each other's company – imagine your work area as simply an extension of your coffee area.

Flexibility

"Whatever is flexible and living will tend to grow; whatever is rigid and blocked will wither and die."

Lao Tzu, philosopher

Improvisation demands flexibility. The hallmark of an effective leader, now and in the future, is the ability to adjust and respond appropriately to each new situation. Given that situations will nearly always be new, it's pointless to look for 'tick-box' solutions or to try to 'do it by the book'. Our ability to adapt and embrace flexibility is an important reason we have survived as human beings. Unfortunately, as people move into positions of authority and power, this natural capability often becomes compromised. It starts to atrophy, replaced by more rigid thinking and a reliance on systems, procedures and bureaucracies.

Avoid being the kind of leader who shuts down when multiple demands appear. For example, one set of bosses announced to their company that they did not want any more ideas because there were 'too many for us to handle'. Not surprisingly, the supply of ideas quickly dried up. Instead, show you are willing to deal with many demands. This could mean you welcome interruptions during your working day, or maintain a genuine 'open door' policy anywhere – from home to work.

Juggling several initiatives at the same time is likely to become business-as-usual. When faced with multiple and apparently overwhelming demands, you need to be able to:

- **Seek help**: invite others to take on important tasks; ask for help and guidance.
- **Rapidly adjust priorities**: don't treat everything as equally important.
- **Focus on the main problem in front of you**: decide what is urgent and important.

A river finds many ways to reach the sea, going around and through obstacles. Being a flexible leader means doing the same – taking responsibility for using new information and changing circumstances, and finding a fluid and often innovative response.

> "It is not the strongest of the species that survives, nor the most intelligent, it is the one that is most adaptable to change."
>
> Charles Darwin, naturalist

Presence

Presence is your ability to bring your full attention and awareness into the moment. In the 'now' there is no past or future – only possibility. It is a moment of pure potential. Instead of concentrating on what has already happened, or worrying about and anticipating what might occur, you are free to improvise and spontaneously produce whatever you want, right now.

These days, presence is also sometimes described as 'mindfulness'. In this you develop awareness of everything that is going on around you, as well as what is going on within you. At Maynard Leigh, we have been showing leaders how to increase their presence for many years. You can learn to reflect more on what is happening in the moment, by asking such questions as:

- What is happening right now?
- How am I feeling in this moment and why?
- What do others feel now and why?
- What is *not* being said?
- What is the body language of people telling me?
- What ideas are coming to mind at the moment?
- How are others performing right now?
- What is the performance data telling me?
- What needs to happen to change the dynamic around me?
- What do I want to create – right now?

Listed here, these may look fairly straightforward. In practice they prove challenging to unravel. Such questions have long been a blind spot in what actual leaders do. If you can be present and bring your full attention to any situation, you are far more likely to be able to improvise and innovate.

Being present helps you to ignore preconceptions and old ways of making sense of what is happening. It involves letting go of certainties, along with the need to control, and instead allowing fresh conceptions and ideas to surface.

Physical presence

Simply being there makes a difference. Not only do you 'see' what is needed in that moment, you are also open to fresh information. Three months after being appointed chief executive of the mining company Anglo American, Cynthia Carroll insisted on visiting the group's largest platinum mine and seeing for herself what it was like two kilometres underground. While there, she was told how dangerous and deadly the mine was, and instantly closed it. 'It was a big wake-up call,' she says.

As you advance in an organisation, you can easily become isolated, locked away in an executive suite, relying almost entirely on others to tell you what is happening. You can, however, make a conscious effort to stay present, to value moments when you can interact with colleagues and learn how performance can be improved. Many progressive companies encourage 'back to the floor' initiatives to keep senior leaders in touch with what's going on.

DaVita, specialists in medical devices, requires key officials to do front-line stints so they stay in closer touch with their troops. Middle managers and executives must also shadow employees in other roles, such as dietician and social worker, for at least one day a year. Vice-President Carolyn Kibler in the US division went on dialysis duty, and found it sharpened her awareness that 'even minor management decisions affect patient caregivers. I truly understand the challenges our front-line teams face every day,' she explained. 'It's like a layer of my skin.'[7]

The future will almost certainly depend on leaders who stay present and enhance their awareness by taking the trouble to visit different sites regularly, speak in depth to staff and suppliers, offer question-and-answer sessions and generally stick around physically. It's a great way of collating and sharing best practice.

John Timpson, who built the national UK chain of shoe repair and service shops, regularly visited his stores. In one case he saw the Cheadle shop displaying a whole line of leather goods on the rack above the machinery. He found that the manager there repaired more leather-soled shoes than anyone else in the business, yet his shop was in a small suburb of Manchester. Timpson encouraged every other branch to adopt a similar display of leather items and 'in the next eight years our leather business quadrupled. No wonder it's called "walking the talk"'.

[7] J.S. Lublin, 'How to be a better boss? Spend time on the front lines', *Wall Street Journal*, 9 February 2012.

Psychological presence

The ability to improvise starts with bringing your full attention – both heart and mind – to a situation. Being distracted, aloof, and showing little interest in what is happening around you will not only rob you of crucial information, it will also evoke a similar approach in those you lead. Being present emotionally and psychologically means you are intensely alert to what is happening around you. It's much the same way a martial arts practitioner becomes acutely aware of the surroundings and what others are doing and thinking.

How do you become emotionally or psychologically present?

- You become entirely focused on *seeing*. That is, you constantly look around at what's happening in the moment. It's what good actors do when they stay fully present on stage, even though they have no lines to speak or actions to keep them busy.
- You *listen* intently, without constantly planning what to say when your turn comes. Instead, you listen with a clear purpose, mentally checking: 'What am I hearing?', 'What have I seen?' 'How will what is happening move us on?' 'How can I contribute to that?'
- You allow your *feelings* to guide your responses and actions. By staying in touch with how you are feeling in this moment, you uncover information about how to improvise.
- You act as if every single moment is different and an opportunity to move the business on.

A useful shorthand version of this process is: *see, listen, feel*. Each sense adds to your ability to improvise.

TWITTER SUMMARY

Change requires a creative response – you can't carry on with what you've always done. You need to improvise new solutions and approaches.

RECAP

Leadership improvisation is your ability to create, innovate and make it up as you go along, without always relying on complete plans. Improvisation depends on a mixture of creativity, flexibility and presence.

IDEAS FOR ACTION

- ✔ Explore what makes you creative through discovering: How do I best tap my natural creativity? What triggers my creativity? When do I get my best ideas? How do I usually respond to other people's creativity? How often do I take regular time for reflection?
- ✔ Use team meetings to explore creativity together. Whether it is brainstorming to tackle a problem, or other creative techniques, every meeting can be a laboratory of invention.
- ✔ Communicate clearly that you have faith in people's innate ability to achieve breakthroughs.
- ✔ Demonstrate that you want to learn through experimentation – by 'modelling' such behaviour you help others to see the importance of it.
- ✔ Practise giving a 'Let's try it and see' response when people produce ideas – much better than a 'Yes, but …' response.
- ✔ Underpin people's freedom to experiment by responding to mistakes as invaluable opportunities for learning – don't punish

people for failure where they have tried to make something work, and stress that the only unacceptable mistakes are ones that could 'hole the ship below the water line'.

- ✔ Offer hypotheses for people in the organisation to test. For example, you might suggest that there is a growing market for a new type of service.
- ✔ Regularly use brainstorming, or its equivalent, to produce lots of ideas, without initially criticising or rejecting them.
- ✔ Wherever possible, focus on solutions, not obstacles.
- ✔ Find ways of communicating that swiftly move any new idea from source to where it's needed. Try suggestion boxes, email systems, open communication – anything that ensures that good ideas can be used quickly.
- ✔ See obstacles as opportunities to find innovative and flexible solutions.
- ✔ Practise giving people your full attention, at least for a while.

07

Implement

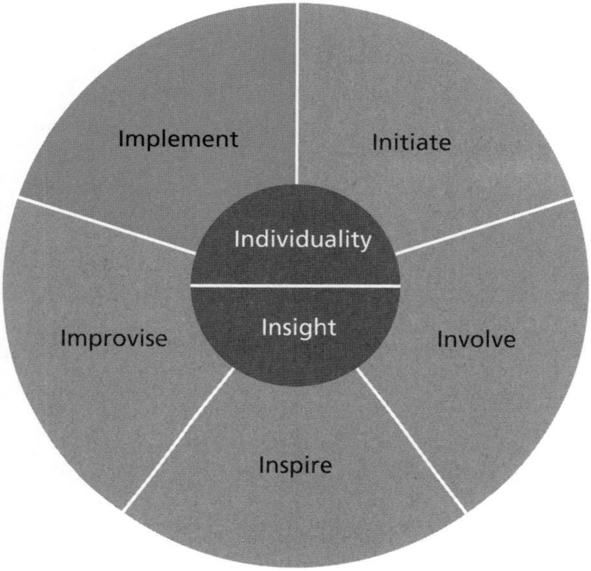

'I always say, "I'm a carpenter, not an architect",' claims Jimmy Wales, who invented and runs Wikipedia. What matters to him is taking action, not just talking about it. 'A big part of what made Wikipedia work is that I just sat down and started doing it, plugging away every day.'

Jimmy Wales is an exception. Nine times out of ten leaders fail to **implement** successfully the strategies they create. They habitually underestimate the challenge of turning their initiatives into action. First, they assume it's harder to create a strategy than implement it. Second, they often delegate the job of implementation to others, consequently taking their eye off what need to be done.[1]

As a leader in the twenty-first century you will be facing forces unleashed by widespread collaboration, networking and distributed leadership. These forces promote change, but also provide

[1] R. Speculand, 'Six necessary mind shifts for implementing strategy', *Business Strategy Series*, 10(3), 2009.

many opportunities to make change hard to achieve. Therefore you need to be action-minded and adept at execution, often against the odds and despite inertia and resistance to change. In these circumstances the difference between success and failure is asking: 'Am I taking the *right* actions?'

Five signs of effective implementation

1 **Strong vision**. Establish clear, practical steps for moving from wishful thinking through to intention and then to on-the-ground action.

2 **Good alignment**. You align people with what they want to do and you watch for small divergences from your intention that can accumulate into outright failure to implement.

3 **Cultural shift**. Much of your effort goes on changing the organisation's culture in order to produce action.

4 **Fast, logical processes**. These are responsive, rational methods that allow the organisation to be nimble and adaptive.

5 **Adequate metrics and feedback**. You know whether you are moving towards or away from your destination and at what speed; you have tangible evidence, not bland assurances.

While past leaders mainly saw implementation in terms of 'making it happen', this is now too narrow a perspective. Instead you will need a long-term view of strategy, being concerned, for example, with sustainability. Previous generations of leaders did not have to worry much about sustainability. But during this century we can reasonably expect this to become an increasingly important issue. For example, can your employees sustain their level of performance long enough to ensure implementation is successful? Sustainability questions you may need to ask include:

- What is the long-term environmental impact of this action?
- Have we access to sufficient resources to keep doing this?
- Is this action likely to be good or bad for people and the planet?
- How will our customers view our actions in terms of ethics and sustainability?
- What are the biggest barriers to sustainability in this instance?
- How might this action help our sustainability credentials?

Be action-minded

"If you don't commit – you're just taking up space."

Dame Stephanie 'Steve' Shirley, IT entrepreneur and philanthropist

What makes *leading the way* an almost unstoppable process? Typically it's when you, as a leader, are obsessed with making things happen and seeing them through to completion. Visions and plans are often there aplenty, but they are meaningless unless you push hard for them to be made real. When you demand deeds not just words, you are being action-minded.

People need to know not merely the vision, the plan and the destination. They also want to know: 'What do you need *us* to do to get us there?' Being action-minded requires you to spell out for everyone their distinct part in making what you want happen. When a cleaner at Boeing, who was responsible for keeping washrooms pleasant, was asked 'What's your job?' he reportedly replied: 'I'm helping to build a 707'.

Paralysis of analysis

R.J. Hildebrand, a 23-year-old rookie driver, was poised to win the 2011 Indy 500 race. On the final lap, tragedy struck. As he made the final turn, comfortably in the lead, he lost control of his car briefly, slammed into the wall and was passed by another driver. This shocking turn of events startled viewers and analysts. How could someone, having made 799 left turns successfully, then on the 800th one, with only seconds separating him from victory, make such a costly mistake?

Nobody knows what went through Hildebrand's mind as he fouled up, but almost certainly the cause was thinking too much. Previously, he took for granted the whole business of turning. Now though, as victory was almost within his grasp, he stopped being 'unconsciously competent' and instead, thinking of the impending victory, he became consciously incompetent.

Quite simply, Hildebrand suffered from paralysis of analysis – and many organisation leaders experience it too. 'We need more information' is a frequent cry of leaders who prefer not to make a hasty decision. They believe that if only they can obtain just a bit more data the difficult choices will become easier. The result is too much time spent on collecting and analysing data, so nothing actually gets done. The classic case where this occurs is Hamlet, who thinks too much: his youth and vital energy, in Shakespeare's words, 'sicklied o'er with the pale cast of thought'.

Resist making things over-complicated and focus instead on keeping things simple. With too many options, a choice is always avoidable, so prioritise.

Seven ways to see off analysis paralysis

1 **Plan**. You need a plan but beware over-planning; decide what you must know before you start, as opposed to what it would be nice to know. Nail down what could go wrong and try to prevent it.

2 **Set a deadline for planning**. Limit your planning and be strict about ending it. The more time you devote to planning, the longer you will take!

3 **Just start**. Every journey begins with a single step. What's yours – apart from yet more planning? Stop asking 'What if?' questions and act, learning everything you need along the way.

4 **Abandon perfection**. It's not possible to have everything perfect – the law of unintended consequences will see to that. Just start taking action.

5 **Maintain the momentum**. Once you start, don't stop and think too much again. Keep a list of to-do items and work through them – no matter how big or small the task.

6 **Hone your decision making**. Knowing how to make faster and wiser decisions will let you take action faster and get more things done. Practise your decision-making skills by setting deadlines for all kinds of small decisions.

7 **Find an action taker**. Link up with someone good at taking action – talk to them about your issue and you'll probably get a positive reply and the momentum needed to get going.

Setting goals

You would have to be an odd leader not to set goals. But *leading the way* requires more than mere selection of goals and trying to implement them. You need to examine what sort of goals you are setting. In today's environment you need to have goals that are not average or pedestrian. Studies into the human drive to achieve[2] offer you useful pointers for setting goals under these demanding circumstances – as outlined in the box.

[2] See, for example, D. McClelland, *The Achieving Society*, Simon and Schuster, 1967.

The psychology of achievement-driven people

- Achievement is more important than material or financial reward.
- Achieving the aim or task gives greater personal satisfaction than receiving praise or recognition.
- Security is not a prime motivator, nor is status.
- Feedback is essential, because it enables measurement of success.
- These people constantly seek improvements and ways of doing things better.
- They will logically favour jobs and responsibilities that naturally satisfy their needs.

How do you set extraordinary goals that inspire and get people's juices flowing? This has puzzled even talented leaders. Many have mistakenly chosen unreachable ones. For example, the chief executive of one major corporation set the goal of increasing profits every year by 10 per cent. In the short term this was manageable; in the long run it became an impossible burden – the ludicrously ultimate implication was that one day the company would employ the entire population of the country!

With an eye on strong execution, goal setting therefore poses a number of questions, including:[3]

- What makes a good goal?
- Should goals be short-term or long-term?
- Should goals be lofty or practical?
- How do you know if a goal is realistic?
- How many goals should you have at the same time?

[3] For useful answers to these questions, see mygoals.com help centre.

- What if goals conflict with each other?
- How should you prioritise goals?
- In how many categories should goals be set?
- What do you do if you have an idea for a goal, but are not sure where to begin?
- Does there need to be a reason for having a goal?

You can answer some of these dilemmas by making sure goal-setting is a collaborative affair, involving those who will be expected to achieve the results. After all, those who take part are those most likely to work hard to reach the result and most likely to feel passionate about succeeding.

Sometimes, though, it makes sense to impose a goal and leave little room for people to alter or challenge it. When President Kennedy famously announced that he was committing the US to landing a man on the Moon within a strict timetable, he was not asking, but telling. Nevertheless this inspiring aim clearly galvanised and excited a mass of people. Dictating goals can work if they genuinely do affect people emotionally, so they respond positively to the challenge.

> "Whether you think you can or you think you can't, you're probably right."
>
> **Henry Ford, founder of the Ford Motor Company**

SMART goals

Setting SMART goals is a well-tried way of bolstering the implementation effort, which brings discipline to planned action. There are many versions of this acronym. We use the one we devised some years ago, which has proved very effective:

- **Stretching**. Excite a person to strive for new performance or development levels; a person's reach should exceed their grasp – unchallenging goals seldom work.[4]
- **Measurable**. Make goals specific so that you know whether or not they are achieved and at what rate.
- **Agreed**. Make goals realistic and accepted by those who have to achieve them; imposing goals on people occasionally works but generally proves ineffective.
- **Recorded**. Keep track of progress so that you know what is supposed to be achieved by when and by whom.
- **Time limited**. A goal with no time boundary is a goal without hope. People need to work to clear, understandable deadlines. 'As soon as possible' is not a deadline.

Ten ways to make goals trigger inspiration

1 Demand that goals be exceptional – not just 'average' or more of the same.

2 Link goals to what people really care about in their life.

3 Keep asking: 'Are you working towards this goal right now?'

4 Break large goals into manageable chunks.

5 Build detailed action plans around each goal.

6 Monitor progress relentlessly, without undermining trust.

7 Regularly review goals to clarify expectations, adjust difficulty and gain recognition.

8 Ensure important goals achieve a high profile, including who has committed to them.

[4] This goal is sometimes defined as Specific, but if a goal is measurable then it is almost certainly specific; we have found Stretching a more useful criterion.

9 Benchmark opportunities or targets, so individuals see for themselves how they're doing.

10 Recognise effort and celebrate the achievement of steps towards the goals.

Monitoring progress

Implementation without monitoring progress makes little sense. *Leading the way* demands a continual awareness of the bigger picture. This requires milestones and deadlines to keep up the momentum. You may need to keep asking yourself questions such as:

- How are things going?
- What obstacles have we hit?
- When will we reach our aim?
- Are we still on target?
- How close are we to our goal?

You can inject a sense of urgency into your monitoring by regular progress-type questions, such as the ones above, and also about specific events:

- What happened after we talked last week?
- Is the project now under way?
- Have we made that recruitment decision?

One important tip about making monitoring work is to do it in an interested way, not in a spirit of checking, or being inquisitorial. Rather than pestering people and showing you don't trust them, communicate your curiosity and your wish to stay in touch. After all, if you don't ask these questions, how can people expect you to be able to offer support?

Many organisations are cluttered with numerous initiatives that lack clarity. This affects attitudes, morale and people's sense of direction or purpose. Incomplete projects sap energy simply by hanging around, demanding attention. Instead:

- Set definite deadlines for finishing.
- Make clear to everyone that deadlines mean what they say.
- In your area of responsibility, root out dead, dying or irrelevant projects and scrap them.
- Check the physical space you and your team occupy, removing clutter, hardly used equipment, papers 'pending', and knick-knacks that seem to make the space personal but which just add disorder.

Ask for help

"It marks a big step in your development when you come to realise that other people can help you do a better job than you could do alone."

Andrew Carnegie, US industrialist

DIY disasters cost bungling Brits £2.1 billion a year, according to a 2011 study. Around 42 per cent of people said they had caused so much damage by bungling home improvements they wish they'd hired a professional tradesperson before attempting jobs.[5] The desire to go it alone is widespread and there are even entire TV channels devoted to avoiding professionals and instead doing it yourself. But *leading the way* does not mean going it alone. Successful implementation relies on being willing to ask for help.

[5] Newslite.tv, 2 May 2011.

For some leaders asking for help feels difficult, in case it seems an admission of weakness. To be successful, you need to be less precious about seeking help. Stop worrying about appearances and start seeking aid from others. Help supports you and it also makes your helpers feel valuable. People get a boost from sharing knowledge or offering expertise. Being able to contribute gives them a sense of accomplishment and affirms their worth. The bottom line is that people have a universal need to be needed. So you might as well tap into their energy and generosity.

Model behaviour

"Example is leadership."

Albert Schweitzer, philosopher and recipient of the Nobel Peace Prize

Bill Hewlett, co-founder of Hewlett-Packard, once broke open a lock on a store room cupboard and placed it on a manager's desk along with a note. The note read that the locked store room did not reflect the HP value of respect for employees. He was saying 'Trust them'. By modelling desired behaviour, Hewlett was bringing to life the values he held so dear. No matter how genuine and moral your values, or how well articulated they are, people need to see you 'living them'. Only then will they understand the spirit behind them and the significance of what you want to achieve.

According to Towers Perrin research in 2007, most (80–90 per cent) of the behaviour of others is determined by:

- What leaders attend to, measure, reward and control.
- The leader's reaction to critical incidents.
- The leader's role-modelling behaviour.[6]

[6] R. Able, *The Importance of Leadership and Culture to M&A Success*, Towers Perrin, 2007.

Across the entire field of leadership there seems general agreement on the importance of modelling behaviour. Countless studies and the personal experiences of leaders themselves confirm that leadership is not about who you are or where you come from. It's about what you do. Your behaviour explains why people feel engaged and want to implement your plans. What you *do* proves many times more important than any individual or organisational characteristic, such as charisma, courage, persistence, business know-how and so on.[7]

Modelling desired behaviour has always been an important requirement for leaders, and this will be accentuated in the future. In fact the ability to 'walk the talk' will be a major test of leadership. In so many situations you will not have the power your predecessors once exercised to make things happen. Asking people to do something you are unwilling to do yourself will therefore be a sure way to undermine your implementation effort. Modelling speaks louder than words; its power achieves far more than exhortation.

"Leaders must be seen to be upfront, up to date, up to their job and up early in the morning."

Lord Sieff, former chairman of Marks & Spencer

Quite simply, modelling separates ordinary leaders from those who inspire. Toby Ord is an academic who set up the charity Giving What We Can. Each member of this widely expanding global network signs the following pledge:

I recognise that I can use part of my income to do a significant amount of good in the developing world. Since I can live well enough on a smaller income, I pledge that from today, until the day I retire, I shall give at least

[7] See, for example, J. Kouzes and B. Posner, 'Ordinary people, extraordinary results', *Talent Management Magazine*, December 2011.

ten percent of what I earn to whichever organisations can most effectively use it to fight poverty in developing countries. I make this pledge freely, openly, and without regret.[8]

Making such a commitment is a serious ask. However, its founder – an academic earning not much more than the average salary – is *leading the way* by donating at least a third of his own income. 'I realised that by donating a large part of my future earnings to the most efficient charities, I really could save thousands of people's lives. Since I already have most of the things I really value in life, I thought – why not?' His personal modelling has encouraged many more high-net-worth individuals to do the same, and the current level of pledging that Giving What We Can has facilitated is over $700 million. Ord is the embodiment of the phrase 'Putting your money where your mouth is'!

Seek feedback

Chapter 4 looked at the sort of feedback needed to involve people. However, nearly all successful leaders hunger for feedback about their attempts at implementation. In twenty-first-century organisations these leaders are relating to ever more people and far more complicated arrangements than their predecessors. With flatter hierarchies, more collaborative working and an emphasis on diversity of talent, virtual teams and other technology-based developments, they need to master a wide range of feedback.

Feedback has always been challenging for leaders and can certainly be a double-edged sword. While it can help clarify whether your leadership is making things happen, feedback can also be highly confronting when things do not go well. If you are emotionally intelligent you can cope with this downside by staying open. You

[8] www.givingwhatwecan.org/our-pledge

need to avoid taking the resulting information as a personal attack and, therefore, avoid reacting so that others feel penalised.

You can expect to access two distinct kinds of feedback sources about your efforts at implementation: personal feedback and organisational feedback. Both are essential for your success.

Personal feedback

The power of personal feedback was shown dramatically in the UK with the 2010 release of information about individual success rates of heart surgeons. Since then, UK death rates from heart surgery have fallen significantly. Prior to this feedback, the lack of evidence allowed less competent people to hide behind a blind spot.

Blind spots are the single best predictor of low performance appraisal ratings. They can result in many destructive leadership behaviours, including defensiveness, lack of humility, insensitivity, and a tendency to be over-controlling or overly assertive.[9] Failing to recognise your blind spots early in your career can damage your prospects as a leader. If you don't address them before moving up the career ladder, when you finally reach a higher-level position you may be unaware of them because you are less likely to receive honest and direct feedback.

You can extract personal feedback from a variety of sources, including:

- informal conversations
- formal sessions, such as performance reviews
- employee opinion surveys
- one-to-one coaching
- mentoring.

[9] J. Evelyn Orr *et al.*, *Illuminating Blind Spots and Hidden Strengths*, Korn Ferry Institute, 2010.

Informal conversations can be particularly helpful when you are clearly open to hearing both good and bad news. A chat round a coffee machine, for instance, may tell you much about why a favoured project is running into the sand.

Organisational feedback

This kind of feedback stems from sources such as:

- formal metrics
- systems and procedures
- customers
- surveys
- investors.

However, organisational feedback needs to be carefully refined. It is easy to be swamped with information that ends up being ignored, wasted, or both. Never be afraid to challenge the worth of this kind of feedback if it does not make your job easier. Key performance indicators, for example, will only be useful if they actually shed light on whether implementation is moving in the right direction.

The data, however, is only the first step. You will need to interpret it and then act on its findings. Numbers on their own are neutral. For them to have any meaning, you need to look for the relationships between the numbers, and especially any apparent trends. And, once you've made sense of them and what they indicate, you will need to take action. It is amazing how many companies run employee opinion surveys and then ignore the results.

Persist

In 2011 the creators of the Angry Birds game, Rovio Entertainment, announced they had taken $42 million in funding. They currently hold the record for the best-selling phone-based game ever. There is talk of a movie featuring Angry Birds. There is no denying that Angry Birds is a cultural phenomenon, but one thing it's not is an 'overnight success'. The leaders of Rovio spent eight years working on other games before they finally caught a huge break. That takes dedication. For almost a decade, they did not have any big wins.[10]

Successful leaders need sheer obstinate determination to keep moving forward, despite the obstacles. There are no real short cuts to being persistent, but you can certainly get better at it. The Catch 22 about persistence is that you have to persist at it!

The so-called Mr Spock model of leadership is no longer tenable. This is a Vulcan-like coolness, in which decisions are calculated, logical, unbiased and intelligent. Once seen as how to run successful organisations, Spock management, or if you prefer scientific management, is not so much obsolete as inadequate in the current climate. As Gary Hamel, one of the world most influential business thinkers, puts it, the way organisations get things done is out of date. 'Like the combustion engine, it's largely a technology that's stopped evolving and that's not good.'[11]

Leadership persistence only makes sense if you also retain flexibility and resilience. Some of this is learnable, and some depends on who you are and how strongly you believe in what you are trying to achieve. Although no one can tell you which values to pursue, the essentials of persistence in the new era are clear:

- **The road ahead is a long one.** Translating vision into reality requires patience, and seeing the road as a journey, not as a short cut.
- **The best way to travel that road is one step at a time.** Persistence also implies the ability to move at a consistent but

[10] P. Hontz, 'Angry Bird's "overnight success" only took eight years', *The Startup Foundry*, 11 March 2011.

[11] Gary Hamel, *The Future of Management*, Harvard Business School Press, 2007.

slow enough pace that allows you to make adjustments as you're travelling down the road.

- **Pacing is critical**. Like the long-distance runner or the 15-round boxer, persistent leaders realise they must pace themselves. To do everything immediately and upfront will exhaust if not bankrupt their initiatives. They are also focused on sustaining momentum. They make sure they push and sustain their initiative so they never get stuck or give up.

Finding your inner source of persistence is partly a matter of practice combined with a readiness to bounce back from adversity. You cannot exactly learn dogged determination, but you can know where it comes from and practise it. To build your persistence, first build your belief in what you want to achieve.

Principles of persistence

- Be willing to step back and rethink.
- Reframe issues so they can be seen differently.
- Continually ask: 'Is this an obstacle or an opportunity?'
- Find a way when there is no way.
- Be enthusiastic – enthusiasm provides the energy to keep going.
- Trust in yourself – believe that you got it right and that now is no time to give up.
- Accept that you'll make mistakes and must keep learning.
- Remind yourself of the legacy you intend to leave.
- Commit to the hard work of keeping going.
- Tap into your natural well of courage – you have this, you just need to use it.

▶

- Draw on the help of others to bolster your persistence – don't try to do it alone.
- Remind yourself that the most successful people have the most failures.

"Diamonds are only chunks of coal that stuck to their jobs."

Minnie Richards Smith, author

Spot success

Underpinning your implementation efforts must be your ability to 'spot success' – that is, realise when people are doing something right. When you highlight good work, publicise people's achievements and reward their efforts, then guess what? People do more of it. This is why breaking down large goals into more manageable ones, for example, creates many chances for people to demonstrate their contribution and help implement your plans.

Moments of success allow both you and the organisation to learn and develop. To spot success requires you to pay close attention to what is going on in a complex, constantly changing environment. Making sure these instances are properly captured and shared is as much a part of successful implementation as making sure that failures provide lessons.

How to spot success

- Keep asking: 'Do you have any examples of success we can share?'
- In a team meeting say: 'What are you each most proud of right now?'

- Search for success where failure previously occurred: 'What has this taught us?'
- Look for trends, not just one-offs in success: 'What is this adding up to?'
- Ask colleagues: 'Do I have a blind spot in spotting success?'
- Invite people to share: 'What's gone really well here recently?'
- Be curious: 'Why are you so enthusiastic about it?'
- Build on others' successes and ask: 'Could we do the same or better?'
- Invent tomorrow today: 'Can we set the standard that others have to follow?'

"Never doubt that a small group of thoughtful, concerned citizens can change the world. Indeed it is the only thing that ever has."

Margaret Mead, cultural anthropologist

Well-being

There is always the danger that the pressure to deliver outstanding results will make it very hard for you to create balance in your life. The more you take the lead and take responsibility, the more will be asked of you and the more you will have to deliver. You are likely to be somebody who functions well under pressure, but there is often a time when healthy pressure crosses the line and becomes toxic stress. So, you will need to be very careful with how you manage your time and your energy.

The great thing is that, as a leader, you are ultimately in charge. You can determine what you say 'Yes' and 'No' to and how much you take on. You will need to learn how to prioritise and delegate so that you have time to pursue the important things rather than just the urgent ones. More than anything, you will need to have time and space to think and plan. Some people do this best while walking the dog, pacing the room, cycling, doing the ironing, or simply sitting. Whatever works for you, make sure you create the space to do so.

The author J.K. Rowling, whose Harry Potter books have become a multi-billion-pound industry, received inspiration on a train journey from Manchester to London. She says it was as if Harry walked down the aisle of the train and into her imagination. She had nothing to write with at the time and so just sat there and thought through the ideas. By the end of the journey she had mapped out all seven books. What would have happened if instead she had been busily responding to emails on a mobile device?

"A significant number of big-money ideas have occurred to me while on vacation."

Nolan Bushnell, founder of Atari

Many of your best ideas as a leader will come while not working frantically to deliver results. You need to look after yourself and ensure you don't get burnt out and that you have a healthy lifestyle with plenty of space for reflection, recovery and revitalisation. And those brilliant ideas!

TWITTER SUMMARY

After all is said and done, more is said than done! Initiatives only add value if they are put into action. So the seventh 'I' is implement.

RECAP

Implementation consists of being action-minded, modelling desired behaviour, giving and receiving feedback, persistence and an ability to spot and celebrate success

IDEAS FOR ACTION

- ✔ Give more attention to direct action than just talking about it. Be willing to devote apparently limitless energy to ensuring your words are turned into deeds.
- ✔ Share openly and constantly exactly what you want to achieve and what the results will bring.
- ✔ Lead through example, so that you share your vision, promote your values, and show commitment to achieving results.
- ✔ Use meetings to pursue implementation. Your conduct of them sends messages to everyone, so communicate clearly and succinctly, listen to suggestions, be attentive, and make sure that everyone is involved.
- ✔ Ensure that people have the necessary information on which to base decisions.
- ✔ Review your own creative thinking by asking: 'Are my thoughts mainly focused on action?' 'Do I prefer rehearsing history, rather than focusing on the future?' 'Am I willing to question the "rules" or rock the boat?'
- ✔ Try keeping a notebook or electronic recorder by your bedside to capture your random thoughts and reflections for achieving action.
- ✔ This week, try the experiment of tracking how much of your daily communications contain a purpose demanding action, rather than just discussion.

- ✔ Monitor progress by questioning those involved.
- ✔ Keep up momentum by being interested in how people are getting on with the project.
- ✔ Continually review all your outstanding tasks, projects and commitments, and follow through to completion – with a definite deadline – or formally abandon them.
- ✔ Check your physical workspace and remove unnecessary clutter.
- ✔ Show people just *how* an exciting or challenging goal might be achieved. This is by being a coach, a mentor or an adviser.
- ✔ Use SMART goals, which are: Stretching, Measurable, Agreed, Recorded, Time-limited.
- ✔ Goals alone are harder to achieve without regular feedback on progress towards them. Make sure you have both personal and organisational feedback.
- ✔ Break large goals into manageable steps, with milestones that help colleagues realise they are making progress. Ask them to identify these and how they would like to celebrate reaching each one.
- ✔ See how many different forms of feedback you can promote. Look for it from informal conversations, formal sessions such as performance reviews, progress reports, coaching and mentoring.
- ✔ Pat yourself and others on the back when things are going well, not just when you achieve your final goal.
- ✔ Be willing to ask for help to identify instances of success, and then tell lots of people about these.
- ✔ Take time out for reflection and revitalisation.
- ✔ Stick at it!

Lead the way – *now!*

Is the *leading the way* approach how leadership will look during the rest of this century? There are already many leaders who exhibit the fundamentals and capabilities of this new dynamic approach to leading. But true exemplars embodying all aspects of what we describe in this book remain harder to find. This shortfall does not mean it's all a figment of our imagination. The emerging organisations of the twenty-first century will ultimately bring the exact nature of *leading the way* into much sharper focus.

Meanwhile, we have plenty of clues about the nature of the new leadership and the demands likely to be placed on you. For example, you must cope with and then master the explosion in social media, the rapid expansion of collaborative working, changing demography, ever more technological challenges, the requirement to leverage learning, expectations about corporate social responsibilities, the impact of emerging markets and the relentless growth of true global competition.

> "It is no longer good enough to do your job well, satisfy customers and generate financial returns … companies will be assessed not only on immediate results, but also on longer term impact – the ultimate effects their actions have on societal well being."
>
> **Rosabeth Moss Kanter, Professor of Business Administration, Harvard Business School**

Against this challenging background there is a growing realisation that old models of how organisations work are obsolete. This leaves many otherwise excellent leaders struggling to make sense of how to make things happen. For example, there is the widespread acceptance that a less mechanistic, non-hierarchical approach to managing organisations is probably the only viable response to these emerging trends in the world. Consequently, the organisation must be treated as a complex adaptive system. This means you will need to influence rather than 'manage' change, negotiate action rather than simply dictate it, and improvise rather than make endlessly detailed plans.

Innumerable surveys across the world report employee alienation and low engagement levels. These can no longer be ignored if you are genuinely concerned with performance. There is a demand for a more holistic and insightful leadership than in the past. For instance, as a new leader you need to adapt by ensuring that the work environment is humane, and that work is meaningful. Failure to do so will leave your organisation vulnerable to those who *do* adapt to changing demands. Talent will simply drift away from such adverse work environments and we will continue to hear plaintive cries deploring the so-called war for talent.

This book is not a manual of how to lead. That remains to be written when the twenty-first century is more fully in focus. Instead, it offers more of a route map, signposting some of the important destinations of your journey. It is a starting point, and we hope you will become the author of your own volume as you experiment and learn from your leadership journey. You will find your own unique ways of doing things – your own set of principles and wisdom.

Our world needs leaders. The planet and the people who live here are in dire need of people with the imagination and inspiration to create a better world. You can personally make a difference by *leading the way*. Right now!

Overview

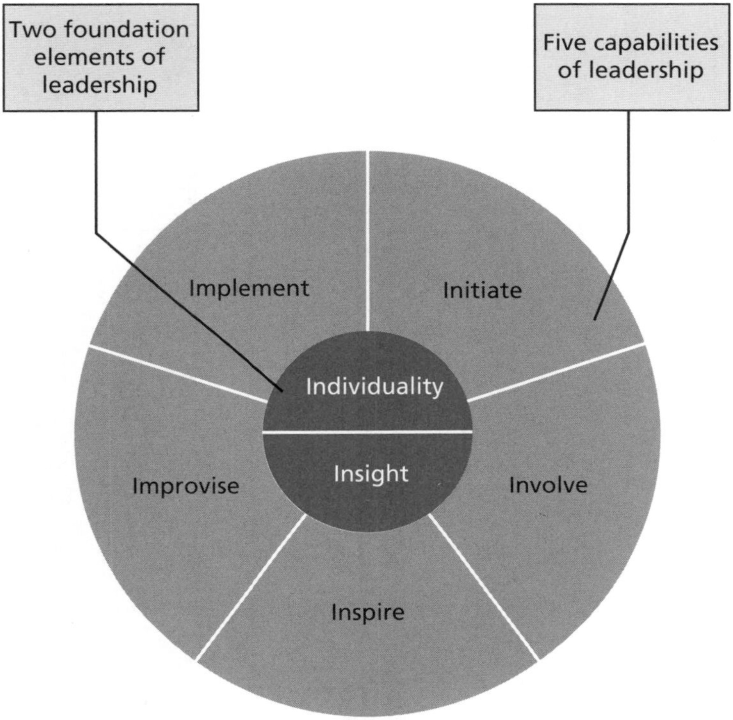

The seven skills to engage, inspire and motivate

Foundation elements

Individuality	Insight
The genius syndrome	Self-awareness
What price charisma?	Understanding other people
The source of individualism	Seeing what's going on
Personal values	
Integrity	
Networking	

Capabilities

Initiate	Involve	Inspire	Improvise	Implement
Accept responsibility	Intensity of involvement	How to inspire	The drive for improvisation	Be action-minded
Research	Participation and enrolment	Vision	The principles of improvisation	Model behaviour
Take risks	Why engage?	Communicate	Creativity	Seek feedback
Instigate direct action	How to engage	Trust	Flexibility	Persist
Follow through	Meetings	Challenging goals	Presence	Spot success
	Empowerment			Well-being
	Coaching			
	Give people a voice			

Are you leading the way?

Time for a reality check. Just how close are you to *leading the way*? What changes to your leadership performance might you need to make to move in the right direction? Great leaders are constantly curious about their own effectiveness and welcome feedback that might help them perform even better.

It can take a dose of courage to willingly explore the issue of your own effectiveness as a leader. Yet the results can be most rewarding by providing a tighter focus on where to concentrate your development energies. A useful approach is to conduct a 360-degree feedback process. First, you complete a self-assessment – you make a judgement on how effective you are on various aspects of the seven Is. Next, you need to invite other people to say how they experience your leadership.

We provide a self-assessment questionnaire on pages 195–198 in which you rate yourself in two stages against the two foundations and the five capabilities of *Leading the Way*. Here are examples of some of the questions:

- I am always happy and at ease with being who I am.
- I have a distinctive style of leadership that people immediately recognise.
- I know what I stand for and what I care about, and communicate these strongly.

Most 360-degree feedback systems tend now to be online via computer, so putting in your responses and getting back information is quick and easy. Feedback takes the form of comparative charts. The example here is the sort of information a Maynard Leigh leadership profile might produce.

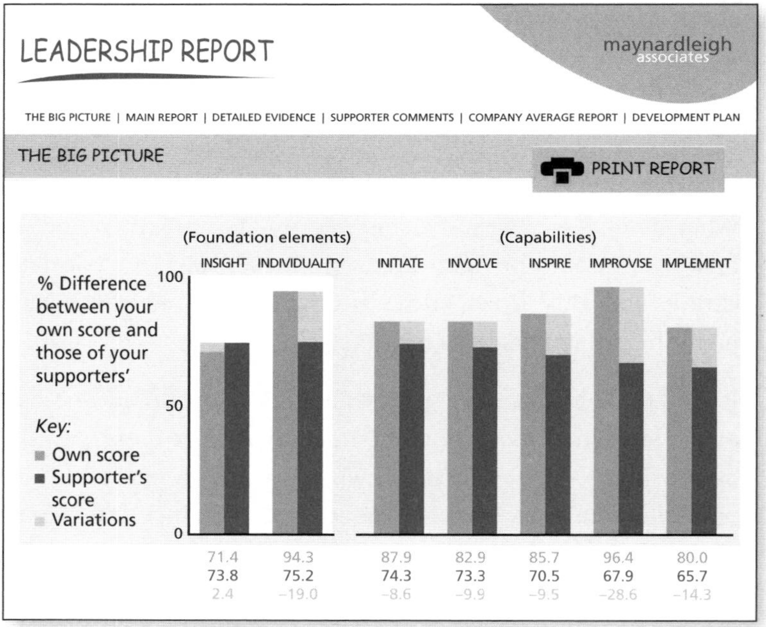

This 'Big Picture' report shows your own score, compares it with how others experience your leadership and highlights the variations. It is these variations that often throw up the most interesting questions. For instance:

- Why do people experience me like that, when I thought they saw me differently?
- Why is the gap between our two perceptions so large/small?
- What factors led to this gap occurring?
- What must I do to change people's perception of my leadership?

It is fairly common for two tendencies to arise when conducting these profile exercises. Either leaders rate themselves more strongly than their supporters do, or vice versa. But where there is close alignment between perceptions, we can be fairly sure you are a leader using your insight. Generally the most revealing information proves to be the difference between one's self-rating and that of supporters.

If you would like to conduct your own leadership profile using feedback from people who experience your leadership, you can do so by contacting info@maynardleigh.co.uk and requesting this fee-based service.

Leadership self-assessment

Foundation elements

Answer each question in this table by disagreeing or agreeing on a seven-point scale: from 1 for disagree strongly to 7 for agree strongly. Which are the areas that need extra work if you want to *lead the way* more successfully?

The highest score possible is 224 and the lowest 32. You can compare your absolute score against ones from your supporters – the calculations are normally shown as percentages and best completed online for accuracy and speed. See chart on page 194.

1	**Individuality**		
	Being yourself	I am always happy and at ease with being who I am.	
	Style	I have a distinctive style of leadership that people immediately recognise.	
	Values	I know what I stand for and what I care about, and communicate these strongly.	
	Integrity	I am seen as truthful, trustworthy and consistent.	

2	**Insight**		
	Self-awareness	I am constantly in touch with how I am feeling and the impact I have on others.	
	Understanding other people	I have a good awareness of what others are thinking and feeling.	
	Seeing what's going on	I am alert to what is happening and the implications for our organisation.	
	Curiosity	I am adaptable and able to handle change.	

Capabilities

3	**Initiate**		
	Taking responsibility	I readily offer to be accountable for achieving something.	
	Risk	I look for opportunities to do new things, even when unsure of the final outcome.	
	Adding value	I promote changes that will make a difference to our business.	
	Vitality	I am sure that people who meet me soon sense my energy and aliveness.	

4	**Involve**		
	Engage	I make sure the people I lead feel valued, involved, developed and inspired.	
	Coach	I regularly use one-to-one coaching to gain the involvement of people at work.	
	Give feedback	I regularly provide people with useful information about their performance.	
	Identify stakeholders	I encourage those with an interest in what I want to achieve to have their say.	

5	**Inspire**		
	Vision	I have a clear picture of what should happen in the future.	
	Communication	I talk openly and clearly about what I think matters.	
	Story-telling	I often bring my communication alive with stories and anecdotes.	
	Passion	I am highly committed and care strongly about what I want to achieve.	
	Trust	I work hard to win people's trust for what we want to do at work.	
	Challenging goals	I make sure people have challenging goals that stretch them at work.	

6	Improvise		
	Creativity	I create a 'try it' environment to encourage inventiveness and fresh thinking.	
	Curiosity	I am always asking questions and exploring what people are feeling and doing.	
	Flexibility	I am adaptable and able to handle change.	
	Presence	I always give people and events my full attention.	

7	Implement		
	Action-minded	I have a reputation for being decisive and making things happen.	
	Modelling	I consistently practise what I preach and lead through example.	
	Seek feedback	I constantly seek feedback about progress towards agreed goals.	
	Persist	I believe in what I want and, despite setbacks, rarely give up.	
	Goals	I set clear, challenging, yet achievable goals.	
	Spot success	I continually look for when people are doing something right or well.	

Recommended reading

Adler, Richard, *Leveraging the Talent-Driven Organization*, The Aspen Institute, 2010.

Bennis, Warren, Gretchen M. Spreitzer and Thomas Cummings (eds), *The Future of Leadership: Today's Top Leadership Thinkers Speak to Tomorrow's Leaders*, Jossey Bass, 2001.

Chartered Institute of Personnel and Development, 'Where has all the trust gone?', 1 March 2012.

Chynoweth, Carly, 'Real chiefs get their hands dirty', *Sunday Times*, 3 October 2010.

Clamps, D., 'Almost ready: how leaders move up', *Harvard Business Review*, January 2005.

Collins, Jim, *Good to Great*, Random House, 2001.

Department of Health, *Staff Involvement: Better Decisions, Better Care*, 2003.

Department of Trade and Industry, *Inspired Leadership: Insights into People Who Inspire Exceptional Performance*, 2004.

Favaro, Ken, Per-Ola Karlsson, Jon Katzenbach and Gary Neilson, *Lessons from the Trenches for New CEOs: Separating Myths from Game Changers*, Booz & Company, 2010.

Goleman, Daniel, 'What makes a leader?', *Harvard Business Review*, January 2004.

Goleman, Daniel, Richard E. Boyatzis and Annie McKee, *The New Leaders: Transforming the Art of Leadership*, Sphere, 2003.

Griffin, Mark A., Alannah E. Rafferty and Claire M. Mason, 'Who started this? Investigating different sources of organizational change', *Journal of Business and Psychology*, **18** (4), 2004.

Gunther, Rita, 'Leadership in a crisis', 29 January 2009, http://ritamcgrath.com/blog

Hamel, Gary, *The Future of Management*, Harvard Business School Press, 2007.

Harvard Business Review Blog Network, 'The role of tomorrow's leaders', 15 September 2010; also www.youtube.com/watch?v=j8WRz3CxafE

Hill, Andrew, 'The art and science of picking a new leader', *Financial Times*, 25 October 2011.

Hill, Linda A. and Hemp, Paul, 'Where will we find tomorrow's leaders? A conversation with Linda A. Hill', *Harvard Business Review*, 1 January 2008.

Institute of Leadership and Management and Management Today, *Index of Leadership Trust*, 2011.

Kotter, John P., *A Force for Change: How Leadership Differs from Management*, The Free Press, 1990.

Kouzes, James and Barry Posner, 'To lead, create a shared vision', *Harvard Business Review*, January 2009.

Krantz, James, 'Lessons from the field: an essay on the crisis of leadership in contemporary organizations', *Journal of Applied Behavioral Science*, **26** (1), 1990.

MacLeod, David and Nita Clarke, *Engaging for Success: Enhancing Performance Through Employee Engagement*, Department of Business, Innovation and Skills, 2009.

Navisys, *The Case for Increasing Employee Engagement*, Navisys Transformation, 2007.

Nielsen, Jeffrey S., *The Myth of Leadership: Creating Leaderless Organizations*, Intercultural Press, 2004.

Nonaka, Ikujiro and Hirotaka Takeuchi, 'The big idea: the wise leader', *Harvard Business Review*, May 2011.

ScienceDaily, 'What makes a good leader: the assertiveness quotient', 5 February 2007.

Semler, Richardo, *Maverick! The Success Story Behind the World's Most Unusual Workplace*, Random House, 2001.

Index

accountability 74, 75
achievement-driven people 170
ACS 151
action-focused coaching 109, 110
action-minded leadership 69, 82–4, 167–75
action-takers 169
agendas, meeting 103
Airey, Dawn 81
analysis paralysis 167–9
Angelou, Maya 28
Anglo American 158
Angry Birds game 179–80
Apple 21, 146
Arcadia 21
Armstrong, Franny 83
assertiveness 81
authenticity 24–5
authoritarian/autocratic style 30, 31
Avon products 151

'back to the floor' initiatives 159
Balon, Adam 131
Bankhead, Tullulah 150
Barrass, David 96
Beckett, Samuel 81
being yourself 24–6
Bennett, Bo 70
Bennis, Warren 57, 124
Bloomberg, Michael 109
The Body Shop 21, 62
Bolland, Marc 128
Booz & Company 77
BP 75, 85–6
Bradley, Karen 140
brainstorming 155
Branson, Richard 21, 24, 117, 154
Buffet, Warren 35
'bullpen' open-office plan 109
Burns, Ursula 151
Bushnell, Nolan 184

capabilities xiv
Carlyle, Thomas 49
Carnegie, Andrew 174
Carphone Warehouse 62
Carroll, Cynthia 158
challenges 79
Change the World at 35,000 ft 84
charisma 22–23, 129
Chartered Institute of Personnel and Development (CIPD) xiv
Christian X, king of Denmark 32
Cicero 77
clarity 129
Clarke, Paul 147
coaching 48, 49, 106–9
  action-focused 109, 110
Collins, Jim 22, 75
comfort zones, stepping out of 78–80
commitment 91, 93
communication 75–6, 95, 100, 128–31
Compaq 57
complex adaptive systems 5, 190
connectivity 6
conversation 130
core capabilities 12–14
creativity 21, 103, 139–40, 145–56
Crozier, Adam 100
cultural shift 166
curiosity 59–61

Darwin, Charles 157
DaVita 159
decision-making 169
delegating style 30, 31
democratic style 30, 91–2
development, personal 101
direct action 82–4
Disney theme parks 96
Disraeli, Benjamin 40
Drucker, Peter 23
Dyson, James 78, 96

Edwards, Tracy 92
Ellison, Harry 146
emerging markets 151
Emerson, Ralph Waldo 25, 51
emotion/feelings 52, 129, 160
emotional challenges 79
emotional intelligence 49
emotional presence 160
empathy 53
empowerment 104–6
engagement 93, 97–101
enrolment 93, 94–6
Enron 11
execution 7, 14, 146

experience, personal 26–8

failure 81–2, 150
FedEx 125–6, 140–1
feedback 58–9, 166, 177–9
  360-degree 193–5
  implementation 166, 177–9
  organisational 179
  personal 47, 111–12, 178–9
feelings/emotion 52, 129, 160
filters 57–9
flexibility 156–7
following through 84–6
Ford, Henry 171
foresight 61–3
Forshaw, Jeff 60
forum theatre 155
foundations xiii–viv, 12
Fox, Mindy 118
Fredberg, Tobias 74
free-reign style 30
Fuller, Richard Buckminster 36
fun projects 155

Gallup 97
game playing 155
Garden Fresh group 46
genius sydrome 20–2
Gerstner, Lou 125
Gillett, Lizzie 83
Giving What We Can charity 176–7
goal setting 132–3, 169–73
Goethe, J.W. von 84, 132
Goleman, Daniel 49
Goodwin, Fred 57, 77–8
Google 127, 147, 148–9
Grade, Michael 25
Graham, Martha 15, 121
Green, Philip 21
Griffin, Jack 11
group facilitation 48

Hamel, Gary 180
Hansberry, Lorraine 29
Happy Ltd 100
Harvey, Eugenie 83–4
Hayward, Tony 75
HCL Technologies 19
health and safety 7
help, seeking 157, 174–5
heroic leader myth 6
Hewlett, Bill 175
Hewlett Packard 11, 175
Hildebrand, R.J. 167–8
Hoffer, Eric 32

IBM 82, 125
ideas 71, 153–4
identity, sense of 25
implementation 14, 165–86
  and action-mindedness 167–75
  and asking for help 174–5
  feedback 166, 177–9
  five signs of effective 166
  ideas for action 185–6
  monitoring progress 173–4
  and persistence 179–81
  spotting success 182–3
improvisation 13–14, 137–161
  and creativity 139–40, 145–56
  and flexibility 156–7
  ideas for action 161–2
  and leadership performance 141
  and presence 157–60
  principles of 142–5
  individuality xiv, 6, 12, 13, 14, 19–41
  charisma 22–3
  genius syndrome 20–2
  ideas for action 40–1
  integrity 35–8
  networking 38–40
  personal values 32–4
  source of 23–32
initiating 13, 69–87
  and accepting responsibility 72–5
  and action-minded leadership 82–4
  and following through 84–6
  ideas for action 86–7
  and researching the situation 75–6
  and risk-taking 77–82
initiative landscape 71–2
Innocent Drinks 131
innovation 146–8
insight xiv, 6, 12, 13, 45–65
  ideas for action 64–5
  seeing what's going on 56–63
  self-awareness 46–52
  understanding other people 52–6
inspiration 13, 14, 101, 117–134
  communication and 128–31
  ideas for action 133–4
  making goals trigger 132–3, 172–3
  sources of 120–2
  trust and 131–2
  vision and creating 124–8
integrity 35–8, 98
internal cast 51–2
involvement 13, 91–113
  coaching 106–9, 110
  commitment 93

empowerment 104–6
engagement 93, 97–101
giving people a voice 109–12
ideas for action 112–13
intensity of 93
meetings 101–3
participation and enrolment 93, 94–6, 106
ITV 100

Jobs, Steve 21, 110
John Lewis partnership 100
Jubilee 2000 campaign 84
Jung, Andrea 151

Kane, Pat 155
Kanter, Rosabeth Moss 137–8, 142, 189
Keller, Helen 121
Kennedy, John F. 171
Kibler, Carolyn 159
Kierkegaard, Søren xiv
Kimball, Miles 149
King, Billie Jean 47
King, Martin Luther 120

Lao Tzu 104, 156
laughter 156
leadership profile 193–5
leadership styles 8–10, 29–32
Leahy, Terry 78
LEGO Group 155
Leigh, Mike 140
Leighton, Allan 128
listening 76, 160
Littlewood, Joan 127
logistics 7
Lush 122

Mack, Michael 46
Madoff, Bernard 36
Mandela, Nelson 121
Marks & Spencer 100, 128
Marx, Groucho 35
Mead, Margaret 20, 183
meetings 101–3
mega forces 5–6
Mercer Consulting 118
metaphors 129
Michelangelo 61
mind-mapping 59
mindfulness 157
MIT Sloane School of Management 142
modelling behaviour 175–7
monitoring progress 173–4
Murdoch, Rupert 21, 39

Navratilova, Martina 91
Nayar, Vineet 19–20
Network for Social Change 84
networking 38–40
News Corporation 21
NHS 97
Nicholson, Nigel 21
Nietzsche, Friedrich 22
Nin, Anais 56
non-personalising 82
Nooyi, Indra 140
Novell company 78

O_2 organisation 100
Obama, Barack 24
observation 54
observe perceive wonder exercise 53–5
Ocado 147
O'Leary, Michael 81
open door policy 109, 156
open-office plan 109
Ord, Toby 176–7
organisational culture 166
organisational feedback 179
organisational structure 71–2
organisations
as complex adaptive systems 5, 190
twentieth-century versus twenty-first-century 4
'out of the box' thinking 143

Page, Larry 148–9
paralysis of analysis 167–9
participation 73–4, 93, 107
participative style 30, 31
passion 122–4
perception 54
performance appraisal 111, 178
persistence 179–81
personal development 101
personal enquiry 50
personal experience 26–8
personal feedback 47, 111–12, 178–9
personal style 28–32
personal values 32–4
personal vision 126
personality profiles 50
Petrobas 126
Pfeiffer, Eckhard 57
physical challenges 79
physical presence 158–9

planning
  deadline for 169
  over- 168
play, culture of 154–6
political challenges 79
post-industrial model of leadership 11
presence 157–60
problem-solving 151–3
  SCAMPER technique 152
prototyping 155
psychological presence 160
psychometric tests 50

Quinn, Robert E. 26

rational thinking 7
recklessness 77
Reed, Richard 131
reframing 82
regulation 7
rejection, dealing with 82
relationship-oriented leadership 8–12
reputation 35
researching the situation 75–6
responsibility, accepting 72–5
risk-aversion 70, 139
risk-taking 77–82, 139, 144, 150
Roddick, Anita 21, 62
role-playing exercises 48
Rolls Royce 152–3
Rosenfield, Irene 139
Rovio Entertainment 179–80
Rowling, J.K. 184
Royal Bank of Scotland 57, 77–8

Sandberg, Sheryl 148–9
SCAMPER technique 152
Schmidt, Eric 78
Schultz, Howard 38
Schweitzer, Albert 175
scientific management 180
seeing 160
self-assessment 47, 193–8
self-awareness 46–52
self-consciousness 50
self-insight 47
self-knowledge 24–6
sensory acuity 63
seven Is of leadership 12–15
Shirley, Stephanie 'Steve' 167
Sieff, Lord 176
simulations 48, 155
Skilling, Jeffrey 11
SMART goals 171–2
Smith, Minnie Richards 182
social challenges 79
social filter 57
social intelligence 53, 55–6
Socrates 120
Soros, George 72
Spock management 180
stakeholders 75
Stanton, Andrew 130
Starbucks 38
story-telling 130
strategic vision 126
Streisand, Barbara 131
style
  leadership 8–10, 29–32
  personal 28–9
success, spotting 182–3
succintness 129
sustainability 166–7

tactical vision 126
taking a stand 38
task-oriented leaders 8, 9
Tchaikovsky, P.I. 118
'temporary' leaders 6
10:10 campaign 83
Tesco 78
31 Ways to Change the World 84
Thompson, Dianne 24
Time Inc. 11
Timpson, John 159
Tomlin, Lily 33
Towers Perrin 97, 175
Toyota 149
Truman, Harry S. 74
trust xiv, 31, 35, 71, 99–100, 131–2, 175
'try-it' environment 148–51

uncertainty 7, 61, 79, 139
understanding other people 52–6
Updike, Vicki 149

values, personal 32–4
valuing people 98–100
VIDI approach 98–101
Virgin 21, 84
vision 124–8, 166
visual imagery 129
volunteering 73

Wales, Jimmy 165
'We Are What We Do' movement 83
well-being 99, 183–4
Wikipedia 165

Wittwer, Reto 28
wondering 54
work-life balance 99
Wright, Jon 131

Xcel Energy 153
Xerox 151

Zaharias, 'Babe' 35

Read on

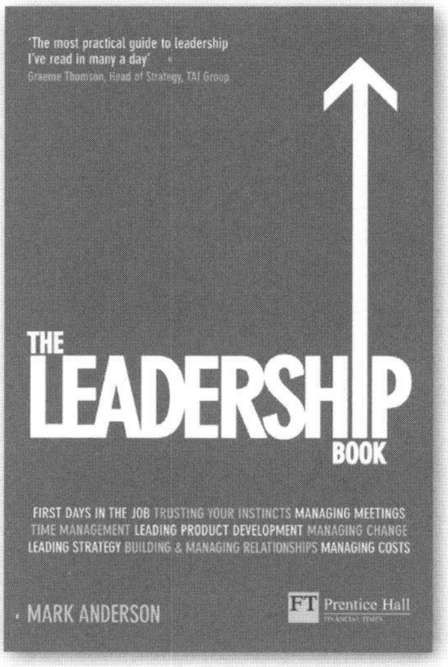

9780273732044

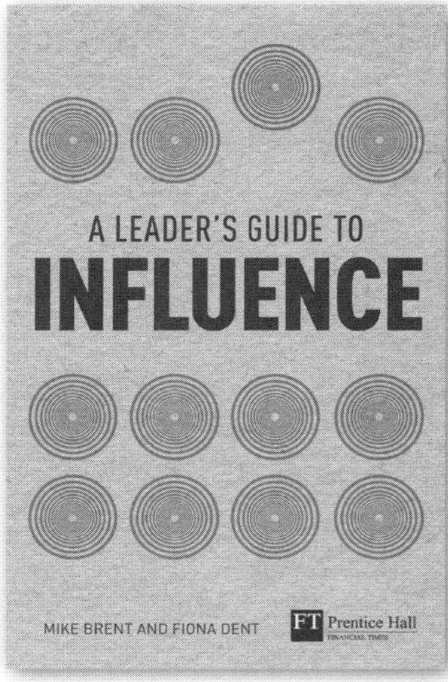

9780273729860

9780273751328

9780273759614

Available now online and at all good bookstores
www.pearson-books.com

ALWAYS LEARNING PEARSON